DRUIDIC SOUL STAR ASTROLOGY

BY:
MARIA WHEATLEY

For permission, serialization, condensation, adaptions, or for our catalog of other publications, write to Ozark Mountain Publishing, Inc., P.O. box 754, Huntsville, AR 72740, ATTN: Permissions Department.

Library of Congress Cataloging-in-Publication Data

Wheatley, Maria – 1964 -

Druidic Soul Star Astrology by Maria Wheatley

A new and exciting way to discover past lives through this branch of Celtic astrology.

1. Astrology   2. Druids   3. Past Lives   4. Metaphysical

I. Maria Wheatley, 1964- II. Astrology III. Metaphysical IV. Title

Library of Congress Catalog Card Number: 2017955625
ISBN: 9781940265469

All planetary images Courtesy NASA/JPL-Caltech.

Cover Art and Layout: www.vril8.com
Book set in: Times New Roman, Lucida Handwriting
Book Design: Tab Pillar
Published by:

OZARK
MOUNTAIN
PUBLISHING

PO Box 754, Huntsville, AR 72740
800-935-0045 or 479-738-2348; fax 479-738-2448
WWW.OZARKMT.COM
Printed in the United States of America

Druidic Soul Star Astrology

Beginnings

*D*ruidic Soul Star astrology is a new and exciting way to discover your past lives without the need for regression. Some people find the idea of past life regression too intrusive and shy away from it. Although past life regression can offer direct understanding of past lives, it is not for everyone – Druidic Soul Star astrology is. Druidic Soul Star astrology is easy to grasp, because it's an intuitive approach based on ancient Celtic wisdom, so you don't need to be an astrologer.

About five years ago, I was standing at the centre of an ancient site near Stonehenge called the Codford Circle. Dramatically situated on elevated ground this earthen circle was once an astronomical Druid temple and it is connected to Stonehenge by a powerful ley line. I closed by eyes and unexpectedly received a psychic-download about Druid astrological practices. I was informed that Celtic astrologers once used a six-pointed star to understand a person's past life and spiritual heritage and that I was once a Druid astrologer and was to show others this ancient art…

The Druid Astronomer said: 'The six-pointed star containing planetary placements was used by Druid astrologers as a spiritual tool for ascertaining information regarding past lives and to understand the Soul's journey through time'.

Over several months, more information came available to me about how to apply Druidic Soul Star astrology and I began to practice this long forgotten star lore. After casting several charts, I soon realised that the details of people's past lives gleaned from a Druidic Soul Star chart seemed highly accurate and resonated with the person. The planets represented their past lives and the chart answered why certain relationship were challenging, why they were drawn to particular countries and generally explained their likes and dislikes. More importantly, it outlines karmic patterns and describes their spiritual heritage. I gave numerous readings and felt they were precise. But was the information that I was giving real? I was about to find out and this Druidic application of astrology was to be put to its ultimate test.

A SPIRITUAL MAP

Druidic Soul Star astrology gives a fascinating insight into past lives and a unique opportunity to work with the light of the Soul. The Druidic Soul Star chart is a spiritual map which describes your past experiences and spiritual heritage, but instead of using a traditional circular astrological chart, which is shown in the illustration, a six-pointed interlacing star is used and certain planets are placed within the star. This new and exciting branch of the astrological tree unites the distant past with the present day.

THE DRUIDIC SOUL STAR

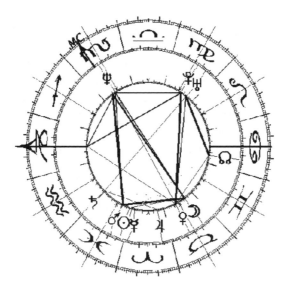

The Druidic Soul Star chart consists of two triangles. The *Soul Star triangle* points upwards towards the heavens; symbolises your soul, important past lives and it connects you to Source. The *Earth Star triangle* points downward representing your personality and connects you to Gaia, Mother Earth. Symbolically speaking, when your first breath was drawn the Heaven and Earth triangles entwined representing the divine union of the personality and Soul.

CELESTIAL GUIDANCE

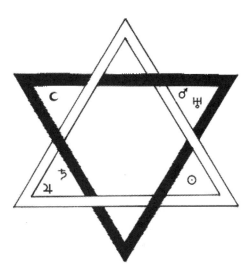

The planet's positions within the star reveal the imagery of your past lives and your karma. Planets in the Soul Star upward point triangle reveal important past lives, karmic rewards and hidden talents whilst planets in the Earth Star triangle describe past lives as well as karmic experiences and their present day consequences.

As we shall see, Druidic Soul Star planets show how karma unconsciously affects our lives by explaining inexplicable fears and puzzling aliments. Mystifying phobias can also be identified, for instance, Neptune can indicate a fear of water and confined spaces invariably due to drowning or imprisonment.

Long forgotten events and experiences are recalled in detail giving vivid descriptions and insights into the distant past. The planets are great cosmic teachers offering us guidance and a deep awareness of who we were and what makes us tick. More importantly, they show us how we can develop latent talents and evolve spiritually.

PLACES WHERE YOU HAVE LIVED BEFORE

The Druidic Soul Star chart also reveals some of the countries and cities where you once lived and experienced strong past life connections.

Unconsciously you may be drawn to visit these places and experience déjà vu as your Higher Self silently reconnects you to the past. Various planetary positions can describe legendary locations. For example, one of Neptune's placements is intimately associated with the lost continent of Atlantis. According to Plato, a philosopher in Classical Greece, at the centre of the Atlantean city there was once a watery shrine dedicated to the God Neptune, Lord of the Seas.

Druidic Soul Star astrology is a practical and spiritual tool. It gives a deep understanding of who you are and gently arouses soul memories of who you were, as time is circular rather than linear and the Soul immortal.

**As we shall soon see, Druidic Soul Star encourages
your intuition to develop, so that you become
a Seer and Karmic Reader of time past.**

Chapter One
Creating A Druidic Soul Star Chart

You will need to access an astrological software programme to calculate a natal birth chart. There are many free on line facilities that allow you to do this. An easy to follow astrological web site which gives the relative information required for a Druidic Soul Star Chart can be found at www.alabe.com I use astrological software called Win Star. For clarity, I will give examples of both software types. However, look around the internet and see what works best for you.

Druidic Soul Star charts are easy to create and soon you will be reading karmic charts for your family, friends or clients.

THE STARTING POINT

Before you can calculate a Druidic Soul Star chart you need an astrological birth chart, which is often called a *natal chart* or *horoscope.* To calculate a birth chart the following personal details are required.

Personal birth details:
•your date of birth   •your place of birth   •your time of birth

If you do not know your time of birth you can use noon or midnight. Using your personal birth details an astrological natal birth chart is calculated, which describes your personality traits. Certain information is extracted from this chart to create a Druidic Soul Star chart, which describes your spiritual traits, psychic ability and your most significant past life experiences.

FROM THE CIRCLE TO THE STAR

Transforming a birth chart into a Druidic Soul Star chart requires just one simple step. You need to determine the astrological *House Position* of the planets and a birth chart provides this information. Do not be concerned with astrological terminology such as *Houses* as this will be explained in detail later. Basically, the celestial zodiac circle of stars in the heavens is divided into 12 sections called 'Houses'. Each House has a meaning, for instance, the First House represents the personality, the Tenth House rules career, and social standing. Unlike astrology, which can take many years to master, Druidic Soul Star is uncomplicated, intuitive and easy to understand.

FINDING THE HOUSE POSITION

Finding the house position of the planets takes a matter of minutes. Below is an astrological birth chart calculated for a woman called Leanne using Electric Ephemeris astrological software and we will transform this birth chart into a past life spiritual chart.

You will notice that on the right hand side of the birth chart a section has been purposely highlighted in grey, which is shown in the following illustration.

LEANNE'S ASTROLOGICAL BIRTH CHART

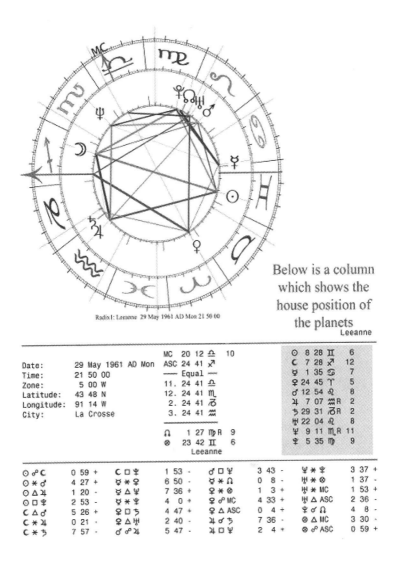

Radix I: Leeanne 29 May 1961 AD Mon 21 50 00

Below is a column which shows the house position of the planets

Leeanne

		MC	20 12 ♎	10	☉	8 28 ♊	6
Date:	29 May 1961 AD Mon	ASC	24 41 ♐		☾	7 28 ♐	12
Time:	21 50 00	— Equal —			☿	1 35 ♋	7
Zone:	5 00 W	11.	24 41 ♎		♀	24 45 ♈	5
Latitude:	43 48 N	12.	24 41 ♏		♂	12 54 ♌	8
Longitude:	91 14 W	2.	24 41 ♑		♃	7 07 ♒R	2
City:	La Crosse	3.	24 41 ♒		♄	29 31 ♑R	2
					♅	22 04 ♌	8
		☊	1 27 ♍R	9	♆	9 11 ♏R	11
		⊗	23 42 ♊	6	♇	5 35 ♍	9
			Leeanne				

☉ ☍ ☾	0 59 +	☾ □ ♇	1 53 -	♂ □ ♆	3 43 -	☿ ⚹ ♇	3 37 +
☉ ⚹ ♂	4 27 +	☿ ⚹ ♀	6 50 -	☿ ⚹ ☊	0 8 -	♅ ⚹ ⊗	1 37 -
☉ △ ♃	1 20 -	☿ △ ♅	7 36 +	♀ ⚹ ⊗	1 3 +	♅ ⚹ MC	1 53 +
☉ □ ♇	2 53 -	☿ ⚹ ♇	4 0 +	♀ ☍ MC	4 33 +	♅ △ ASC	2 36 -
☾ △ ♂	5 26 +	♀ □ ♄	4 47 +	♀ △ ASC	0 4 +	♀ ♂ ☊	4 8 -
☾ ⚹ ♃	0 21 -	♀ △ ♅	2 40 -	♃ ♂ ♄	7 36 -	⊗ △ MC	3 30 -
☾ ⚹ ♄	7 57 -	♂ ☍ ♃	5 47 -	♃ □ ♆	2 4 +	⊗ ☍ ASC	0 59 +

The highlighted column shows the planet, its degree position, zodiac sign and *house position*. Only two bits of information are needed - the house position of each planet - and if the planet was in *retrograde motion* at the time of birth. At this stage, disregard the degree position and zodiac sign.

Astrology uses symbols for the planets and signs of the zodiac. For those unfamiliar with astrological symbolism, I have shown the planetary symbol by its name. You may wish to include the asteroid called Chiron. In the guideline interpretation section of this book, Chiron and its incredible cosmic energy is included.

THE HOUSE POSITIONS OF THE PLANETS

List 1

List 2

Planet	Degree		Zodiac sign	House
☉	8	28	♊	6
☾	7	28	♐	12
☿	1	35	♋	7
♀	24	45	♈	5
♂	12	54	♌	8
♃	7	07	♒ R	2
♄	29	31	♑ R	2
♅	22	04	♌	8
♆	9	11	♏ R	11
♇	5	35	♍	9

☉ Sun at 8 degrees 28 in Gemini in the 6th house

☾ Moon at 7 degrees 28 in Sagittarius in the 12th house

☿ Mercury at 1 degree 35 in Cancer in the 7th house

♀ Venus at 24 degrees 45 in Aries in the 5th house

♂ Mars at 12 degrees 54 in Leo in the 8th house

♃ Jupiter at 7 degrees 07 in Aquarius in the 2nd house

♄ Saturn at 29 degrees 31 in Capricorn in the 2nd house

♅ Uranus at 22 degrees 04 in Leo in the 8th house

♆ Neptune at 9 degrees 11 in Scorpio in the 11th house

♇ Pluto at 5 degrees 35 in Virgo in the 9th house

EXTRACTING THE INFORMATION

Looking at **List 1**, the planet appears in the first column and its house position in the last. We read each line horizontally from left to right. Using only the information from the first and last columns, the first line reads: Sun is in the 6th house. The second line reads Moon in the 12th house, the third line reads Mercury in the 7th, Venus in the 5th, Mars in the 8th, Jupiter in the 2nd, Saturn in the 2nd, Uranus in the 8th, Neptune in the 11th and Pluto in the 9th. The planet's degree and zodiac positions are described in full in List 2.

DRUIDIC SOUL STAR HOUSES

We can narrow this information down even further as Druidic Soul Star astrology only uses planets which are located in the *second, fourth, sixth, eighth, tenth and twelfth houses.* Therefore, only six planets in Leanne's birth chart are used the Sun, Moon, Mars, Jupiter, Saturn and Uranus.

Conveying karmic information, the six key planets will reveal the most significant karmic experiences associated with Leanne's former lives depicting her spiritual heritage. Each planet represents an important past life.

RETROGRADE MOTION

Secondly, we need to establish if the planet was in *retrograde motion*. Look again at List 1, if the letter 'R' appears next to the zodiac sign (or in some astrological charts next to the planet) the planet was in retrograde motion at the time of birth.

In Leanne's birth chart three planets, Jupiter, Saturn and Neptune have an 'R' next to the zodiac sign, which means they were in retrograde motion at the time of her birth – appearing to go backwards in the sky - and this will be discussed later.

CREATING A DRUIDIC SOUL STAR CHART

Finally, to complete Leanne's past life chart the six karmic planets are placed within the star. Planets located in the fourth, eighth and twelfth houses are placed in the downward pointing triangle and the planets found in second, sixth and tenth houses are placed in the upward pointing triangle. The planets always remain in the same house position. Therefore, the Sun in Leanne's astrological birth chart was located in the 6th house and so the Sun is placed in the corresponding 6th house within the Druidic Soul Star chart. Mars and Uranus were both located in the 8th house of the birth chart and so they are placed in the corresponding 8th house of the Druidic Soul Star chart. The Moon is placed in the corresponding 12th house and Jupiter and Saturn are both placed in the 2nd house. The chart is now complete.

THE ASTROLOGICAL HOUSES
OF THE DRUIDIC SOUL STAR CHART

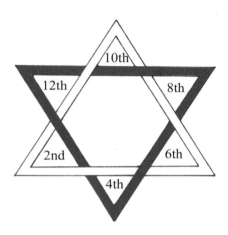

LEANNE'S DRUIDIC SOUL STAR CHART

DESCRIPTION AND KEYWORDS OF THE HOUSES

The Earth Star Triangle 4th, 8th and 12th houses

4th house CANCER – past lives and karma associated with the parents, family members and children Your karmic foundation.

8th house SCORPIO – past lives describing emotional relationships, spiritual and occult wisdom and deep buried emotions. Inherited karmic debts and rewards.

12th house PISCES – distant and ancient karma, karmic fears and aliments. Psychic ability. Metaphysical and occult wisdom and knowledge.

The Druidic Soul Star Triangle 2nd, 6th and 10th houses

2nd house TAURUS– spiritual values and karmic resources. Learning the lesson of money, poverty or riches. A way of harmonising any financial spiritual debts. Learning self love and worth.

6th house VIRGO – spiritual service to others, overcoming karmic blocks and karmic health aliments.

10th house CAPRICORN – spiritual evolution, opening the crown chakra and karmic gifts. Higher consciousness. Off planet incarnations.

USING FREE SOFTWARE

If you are using free software such as www.alabe.com this is what the chart will look like and this is how you extract the information. The company asks that the birth charts should be used for *personal* only. If you want to branch out commercially, I recommend that you buy a good astrological software programme. I use WinStar, but I suggest that you look at various companies and choose which one works best for you. Sometimes free astrological software does not include the House number and so the following charts show how to determine the House positions and numbers.

Chart 1. With No House Numbers

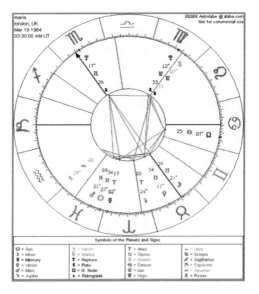

Arrow

shows

House

No. 1

Chart 2. With House Numbers

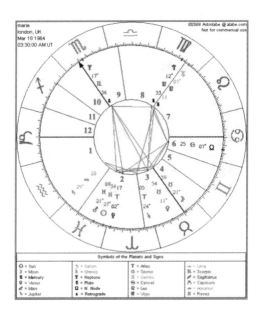

Chart 1 shows no house positions and in Chart 2 I have placed the house numbers in their correct positions. House positions are the dividing lines that create segments.

The houses always follow a specific counter clockwise motion. They always begin on the left and I have depicted this starting position with an arrow. However, as each chart is different and unique, the houses may appear as smaller or larger segments. You can count the 12 houses round by the segments. As some free astrological software sometimes does not include the house numbers, it is good to become familiar with how you can independently calculate them.

The 12 astrological Houses always follow this order, a counter clockwise motion beginning on the left, which is shown in Chart 1 as an arrow.

THE PLANETS WITHIN THE DRUIDIC SOUL STAR CHART

On a higher vibrational level, the planets within the solar system are the keepers of the Akashic Records and like a cosmic library they silently store karmic information. Each planet in a Druidic Soul Star chart represents a past life describing either positive or challenging karma.

Quite often over the duration of time, whilst travelling along the karmic path the same type of challenging situation is met only to be ignored, or repeated, and so ensuring a similar soul lesson in a future life. Soul lessons are always repeated until they are spiritually resolved and these are frequently described by the retrograde planets.

BENEFICIAL KARMIC INFLUENCES

The Sun, Venus and Jupiter often indicate beneficial influences and karmic rewards which have culminated over several lives. The swift moving planets the Moon, Sun, Mercury, Venus and Mars often describe relatively recent karma – that said the incarnation could have been centuries ago!

CHALLENGING KARMIC INFLUENCES

The slower moving planets Jupiter, (Chiron), Saturn, Uranus, Neptune and Pluto invariably describe much older past lives and deep-rooted karma. However, this is a generalisation and you need to take each chart for its own merit. Use your own intuition as the light that guides you.

> **Practice**
>
> Using some free astrological software, extract the relevant information for your own Druidic Soul Star Chart – planets that are in the 4th, 8th, 12th and 2nd, 6th and 10th houses. Make a note if they are retrograde. Mediate upon your Druidic Soul Star or place it under the pillow and sleep upon it. Meditating or simply looking at a Druidic Soul Star Chart can trigger past memories or stimulate your intuition.

RETROGRADE MOTION – SPIRITUAL TRANSFORMATION

When viewed from Earth - from a geocentric point of view - the planets excluding the Sun and the Moon can appear to move backwards in the heavens. This illusory effect caused by the Earth's rotation is called retrograde motion.

In a Druidic Soul Star chart retrograde motion can indicate an important past life or challenging karma manifesting as a difficult or persistent problems, frustrating circumstances, unproductive relationships or phobias. If a retrograde planet appears in a chart, it can represent a challenge and if overcome can offer karmic understanding and spiritual transformation.

I highly recommend that you follow the practical exercises in this book as they encourage you to meditate on the meaning of the Druidic Soul Star houses and the attributes of each planet. More importantly, certain exercises encourage you to make a sacred connection to the planet and this is an important approach according to my Druid Guide. Druidic Soul Star is designed to be intuitive and the karmic interpretations I offer in this book are but *one interpretation* and there are many, many more. Learn to trust your own intuition.

Chapter Two
The Three Sacred Houses
and the Seed of Life

The Druidic Soul Star houses are special. According to the great esoteric astrologer A.G.S. Norris, who wrote *Transcendental Astrology* nearly a century ago, the zodiac signs and houses incorporate the Seed of Life pattern. Norris was aware of this long before the Seed of Life and Flower of Life was made popular.

THE SEED OF LIFE.
THE SEVEN VIBRATIONS OF HARMONY

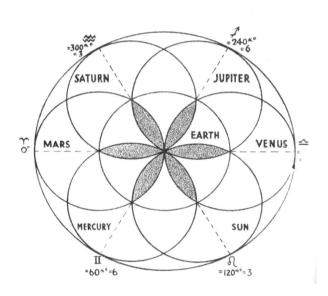

This is the pattern of harmony. The central circle represents the Physical World and the vibration of the Moon. The seven planets orbit and flow around in harmony with the seventh circle of Earth. The three horizontal circles represent the three worlds of matter – physical, astral and mental.

THE LOTUS OR THREEFOLD SOUL

Transcendental astrology teaches us that from the Seed of Astrological Life the spiritual 'Lotus' flower is born.

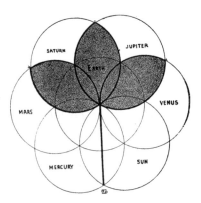

In the darkness of the nadir and within the womb of the Cancer deep within the Fourth House, a stem or the Spiritual Rod has been built. The energy of Uranus awakened the Soul to its inner light. From within this place of darkness, the bud burst into a perfect flower as the Soul reaches perfection. The three petals are the three houses: the 12th on the left, the 10th in the middle and the 8th on the right.

The 10th house is the Crown of Heaven which has transmuted the karma of the 8th and 12th houses. From the physical realm of the fourth house, the spiritual stem was made, and from the inner and outer darkness the Soul seeks the flowering light of love and understanding.

Chapter Three
The Meaning of the Planets - Exploring Their Energy

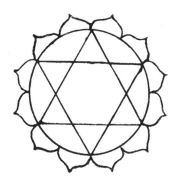

Druidic Soul Star astrology also uses the same symbol that the Yogi use for the heart chakra. It is a timelss Universal symbol that transecends cultures.

For thousands of years, Yogi tradition has depicted the heart chakra as a hexagonal star within a circle surrounded by twelve vermilion petals. The upward pointing triangle of Shiva and consciousness meets the downward pointing triangle of Shakti or force. My Druid Guide says that this was a universal symbol that was used by different cultures worldwide and its Guardians were the Indian peoples of Asia.

The twelve petals can be likened to the twelve signs of the zodiac, each petal representing one celestial lesson. A karmic cycle is complete when the highest virtues pertaining to each zodiacal sign are attained, although this may take many lives to achieve. It is said that the lower chakras, the base, sacral and solar plexus bind the individual to their karma which can be likened to the Earth Star triangle. However, the heart chakra is not subordinate to karmic influences, and according to ancient tradition, when this centre is open universal life is experienced.

On a spiritual level, the Druidic Soul Star chart symbolises the heart chakra and the Soul's astrological journey through time. Understanding the past is the first step towards karmic awareness and freedom, and the Druidic Soul Star chart gives you the opportunity to recognize, heal and release karmic influences that restrict spiritual growth, to open the divine Higher Heart chakra and manifest your highest wish.

PLANETARY INTERPRETATIONS – meet your cosmic teachers and the energies they emit.

Druidic Soul Star interpretation is relatively easy. For an accurate interpretation of a chart you need to know:

• The general attributes of the Planets and the gender they represent.

• The meaning of the six astrological houses used in Druidic Soul Star.

• The combination of the two describes the lives that you lived before this one and your spiritual heritage.

The Druidic Soul Star chart is a spiritual tool; the attributes of the planets may trigger karmic memories for the client as you are accessing the Akashic Records of Truth and Wisdom. You or your client may experience the passing images of former lives, which are often glimpsed by mediating or studying the Star.

WISE TEACHERS

The planets are the Guardians and Teachers of the Solar System and they are related to our Earth Mother, Gaia. Together they are a celestial family. Each planet teaches us a particular evolutionary lesson. For example, the Moon teaches us how to nurture all life forms, that we are emotional and intuitive beings. Mercury teaches the art of communication in all its forms, such as writing, speaking and applying knowledge. The planets can show us our greatest weaknesses and our greatest potentials. We may see the planets as energetic teachers that encircle a high cosmic Light Source–the Sun–whose light bestows life and light upon Earth. The planets are living, breathing life forms that share with us their energy and wisdom.

Astrological scholars have long asked how the ancients came to know the attributes and meaning of the planets. The answer often mooted is that it took centuries of observation to understand the cycles of the planets. Whilst this is true, there maybe a deeper and more profound answer. Could it be that the ancients communicated, or made contact with the consciousness of the planet, which informed humankind of their attributes and influences? It is clear that the ancients employed celestial observational skills as megalithic monuments are aligned to a celestial event, for example, Stonehenge, is orientated to the rising Midsummer Sun. However, in the distant past I think there was an alternative way of astrological-communication that transcends our understanding. Later, we will explore sensitive ways of attuning to the planets.

Let us now look at the attributes of the planets and take our first step towards becoming an adept Druidic Soul Star Past Life Reader. It is worth noting that the planets often give a positive karmic expression and a challenging karmic expression. The querent (client) will relate to one of the expressions or even both. Be guided, as always, by your intuition.

THE SUN

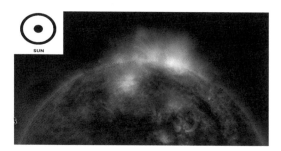

The Sun is traditionally seen as masculine and therefore represents a male incarnation. The Sun's energy bestows a positive karmic influence.

In a birth chart the Sun represents your true self, who you strive to become and how you shine. The Sun is the giver of life, without the Sun we would have no direction, and our lives would be dark and lifeless. The Sun breathes life and light into all living things, and in your Druidic Soul Star chart, the Sun represents positive karma and implies that in a previous life you shone bright and helped others.

The Sun's energy tells us that you once displayed courage, confidence, generosity and loyalty in a life that you lived before this one. The all-seeing turning karmic wheel now grants you general good health or a karmic blessing as a reward.

The Sun indicates deep emotional ties and a karmic bond linking you to a male family member/s. For instance, between the father, son, husband, brother, or a close male friend. You have all incarnated together before and are a part of a soul group or soul family.

Traits that have been carried over into this incarnation are loyalty and courage. You have latent leadership qualities as you once governed people. However, those with challenging Sun karma often feel that they lack the power to lead the way.

In transcendental astrology, the Sun is the highest expression and represents the World of God and its light breathes life into the Solar System and as such gives a Blessing and the ability to heal.

KARMIC HEALTH

The Sun rules the heart, general vitality and the back, especially the spine. The Sun rules the right eye in a man and the left eye in a woman. The Sun has rulership over Leo, the sign that governs the 5th house in the natural zodiac.

THE MOON

*The energy of the Moon is traditionally feminine and
therefore represents a female incarnation.*

The Moon is the fastest moving celestial body, travelling through the
zodiac every 28 days and spending approximately two and a half days
in each zodiac sign.

In a birth chart the Moon rules our needs, emotions, moods and habits.
People with strong Moon energy often have planets in Cancer, show
much sensitivity and are often naturally inclined to nurture and protect
those around them.

The Moon governs our emotions and how we feel about things and
because it influences the tides, it is fitting that it rules all things which
are fluid. The Moon represents the things we want, how we feel about
those things and in turn how they affect us emotionally.

Our emotions set the tone for our daily lives and the Moon's energy
shows us how we are affected by our past memories and how we
process those memories.

In Druidic Soul Star astrology, the Moon is a powerful symbol of
feminine energy representing a life as a woman. It reveals karmic ties
with women, such as the mother, daughter, sister grandmother, aunt or
a close female friend. It suggests that psychic powers are passed down
through the female line and hints at being a priestess in a past life, one
who has previously learnt the ancient art of Magic or Healing.

As the Moon is linked to water it can symbolise an important incarnation where you once lived close to the seas, a river or an island. It also symbolises the growth of the soul in terms of spiritual evolution.

Traits that have been carried over into this incarnation give you a deep connection to the home and family – or the land. You have strong emotions and can sense other people's moods.

You have latent psychic ability. Your spiritual heritage is drawn form ancient wisdom and knowledge from Mystery Schools or the priesthood. Those with strong Moon karma have deep feelings for their children, create a loving environment as they may have lost their home, or a loved one, in a previous life and your Soul Lesson is not to be fearful of loosing those you love.

KARMIC HEALTH

The Moon rules the stomach as well as our gut reactions. It also rules the breasts, the left eye in a man and the right eye in a woman. In transcendental astrology the Moon is associated with the physical world and rules fluids and the etheric part of the aura.

The Moon has rulership over Cancer, the sign that governs the 4th house in the natural zodiac. If the Moon is found in this house in Druidic Soul Star Astrology, it represents a powerful and influential past life.

MERCURY

The energy of the Mercury is traditionally masculine and therefore represents a young man, however, sometimes Mercury energy can manifest as a young woman. Allow your intuition to guide you.

In Greek mythology, Hermes/Mercury was the winged messenger of the gods. Mercury symbolizes all things relating to communication. Mercury governs everything we do to communicate with our voice or written materials, whether it is computers, telephone conversations, books or the media.

Mercury also rules mental energy and language that is concealed such as our ideas, private thoughts and opinions. Mercury never stops collecting data for you and transmits that data to your central nervous system by which your eyes, hands and breathing collaborate.

In Druidic Soul Star astrology, Mercury shows that you were an educated person that liked to travel. You probably spoke a few languages and you were a good communicator. You may have been a trader, merchant, writer, scholar, someone who kept books in a library or someone that once had links to Egypt, the Middle East or Africa. You were clever, well spoken and mentally very quick to think and to act.

Positive inherited traits make you dexterous, clever and quick-witted. Those with strong Mercury energy may be public speakers, writers or researchers. Certainly, you have latent communication skills and writing ability.

You travelled extensively in a previous life and this can influence you today in two completely different ways. Firstly, you may have a desire to travel and experience different cultures. Perhaps as a young adult, you felt it was difficult to settle down or to stick at one job; you like variety and can bore easily. A Soul Lesson is finish that which you start. Alternatively, because in the past you travelled extensively, you now feel that you want to settle down and find your spiritual home.

Challenging Mercury karma can indicate a blocked throat chakra due to trauma such as your opinions were over criticised leaving you feeling mentally inadequate and worthless. If this is the case, you will fear saying what you think and have communication blockages.

In transcendental astrology, Mercury energy acts as a carrier wave of the Solar System that opens the mind to higher realms and dimensions.

KARMIC HEALTH

Mercury rules the lungs, respiratory system, speech impediments and other problems with the mouth and tongue. It also rules the arms, hands, shoulders, the nervous system and illnesses related to them.

Mercury rules the masculine sign of Gemini, the sign that governs the 3rd house in the natural zodiac. Mercury also rules the 6th house sign of Virgo, which is a feminine sign that rules the other functions of the mind that analyzes, defines and discriminates.

If Mercury is found in this Sixth House in Druidic Soul Star Astrology, it represents an important and influential past life.

VENUS

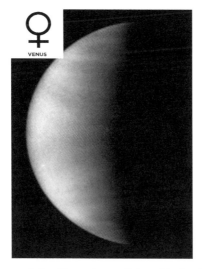

The energy of the Venus is traditionally feminine and represents a female incarnation.

In Greek mythology, Venus was Aphrodite the goddess of love and desire. The word aphrodisiac, meaning that which induces desire, comes from the word Aphrodite.

Venus is feminine energy which rules the world of love, pleasure and all desires. With Venus energy, we experience joy, pleasure, lust and the nature of our own sexuality. Strong Venusian types are lovers of beauty, art, music and food. Venus rules all things related to beauty, from physical attributes to make-up and adornments.

In Druidic Soul Star astrology, Venus shows that you were once a powerful and creative woman. Venus also indicates that you long for your true soul mate, as previously you found one another and the passing of time has not faded that distant memory.

Venus indicates that in a past life you were a loving, affectionate person who was sociable and peaceable. You disliked violence and discord.

Traits that have been carried into this incarnation imply that you may love beautiful objects, and have a real need for peace and harmony.

Marriage and partnerships are especially important to you. You may hate being alone, or fear aloneness and your close friendships are important. This is because you and your close friends are linked to a Soul Group. You are a loyal friend and will help those you love at a drop of a hat. You may have latent artistic or creative talent.

Challenging Venus karma brings social awkwardness, not seeing your own beauty, lustful or selfish energies.

In transcendental astrology, Venus energy develops Divine Thought that is a key which opens the heart to openly express pure love and generosity that knows no boundaries.

KARMIC HEALTH

Venus rules the kidneys, blood sugar and diabetes (Venus rules sugar), as well as illness related to sexual activity.

Venus also rules sensuality and earthly pleasures which are seen through the feminine sign of Taurus which it rules. Venus also has rulership over the masculine 7th house sign of Libra, the sign of partnership. Venus rules over engagements, pairing and unions of all kinds be that romantic or business.

If the Venus is found in this Second House in Druidic Soul Star Astrology, it represents a powerful and influential past life.

MARS

The energy of the Mars is traditionally masculine and therefore represents a male incarnation.

Mars is assertive, powerful and often displays aggressive energy symbolized by Ares the Greek god of war.

Mars is fiery, spontaneous and it can make you brave and fearless. Mars is an action-oriented energy that is in charge of your defences and aggressions and it can cause you to fight back when you are under attack.

Yet, Mars is also the Divine Masculine and it can give you the courage of a bold spiritual warrior that can speak the truth and defend the weak in deed and in word.

Mars shows that in a past life you were confrontational and may have been a warrior as Mars rules strife, combat and weapons. This could have a Knight of King Arthur, the Knights Templar or a Saxon or Dane warrior – let your intuition guide you. It can also imply WWI or WWII energy. Mars rules sharp objects such as swords and knives but guns and weaponry are also associated with Mars.

Mars rules rage and in a past life you were a passionate and powerful man that was fearless but may have been over bearing to others.

Traits that have been carried over into this incarnation are you have strong inner strength and courage but at times you may not act. You can be bold and outspoken and believe in justice and fairness for all.

Any past life wounds from battles or wars may show up as birth marks or reddish patches on the skin.

Mars has rulership over the first house and masculine sign of Aries in the natural zodiac and traditionally it was also associated with the feminine watery sign of Scorpio.

In transcendental astrology, Mars energy represents the astral plain, our desires and emotional body. Mars can be a Divine Sword held by the Spiritual Warrior that cuts through the cord of desire, illusion and unwanted attachments and influences.

KARMIC HEALTH

Mars rules the head, blood and muscles. Aliments such as migraines, injuries to the head, burns, inflammation, fevers and rashes indicate trauma from a past life.

If the Mars is found in this Eighth House in Druidic Soul Star Astrology, it represents a powerful and influential past life.

JUPITER

The energy of the Jupiter is traditionally masculine and therefore represents a masculine incarnation. However, it can sometimes represent a past life as a positive and confident woman.

In Greek Mythology Jupiter was Zeus and it is the largest planet of the solar system, which brings expansion, abundance and growth into our lives.

Jupiter is often described as the Great Benefactor that bestows good fortune, and if it appears in your Druidic Soul Star chart, it shows that you are spiritually blessed as it represents positive karma and a karmic reward. This is because in a previous life you were wise and a generous soul who shared your material wealth with others. You were helpful and came to the assistance of others. Many times you displayed acts of selflessness.

You had a strong spiritual faith and may have been in the priesthood, an astronomer, philosopher or a teacher. Jupiter embraces worldwide cultures and indicates that in a past life you liked to travel and explore distant lands as well as representing someone that was well educated.

In a previous life you displayed fairness and a strong sense of justice and so in this life you hate injustice and despise unfairness.

In transcendental astrology, Jupiter welcomes us to the world of the Divine Spirit and with an open mind it is a key that unlocks the ability to act as a Seer.

KARMIC HEALTH

Jupiter rules the hips, pelvis, liver and the sciatic nerve. It also governs illness where too much of a good thing are contributing factors.

Jupiter has rulership over the masculine sign of Sagittarius, the sign that governs the 9th house in the natural zodiac. Prior to Neptune's discovery, Jupiter also ruled the feminine sign of Pisces.

If Jupiter is found in the Twelfth House in Druidic Soul Star Astrology, it represents a powerful and influential past life.

SATURN

The energy of the Saturn is traditionally masculine and symbolises a masculine incarnation. Occasionally, Saturn can manifest as a wise old woman symbolising a female incarnation.

In Greek Mythology Saturn was Chronos, the god whose name means time. Saturn is known as the Old Man and Father Time. In a Druidic Soul Star chart it points to a meaningful and important past life.

Saturn rules old age, Karma, maturity and time. For centuries, Saturn has long been viewed as evil – Satan – the planet that brings limitations, separations, responsibilities and even death.

Saturn in a Druidic Soul Star chart can sometimes signify karmic duty. Look to the House that contains Saturn, as it will give clues and an understanding of your Karmic responsibility. For example, as we shall soon see, the fourth House represents karma associated with the parents, family members and children. Saturn in this house would show karmic responsibility to family members. It can represent a karmic link to the father, older people and inherited traits from the grandparents. Saturn shows that by excepting your responsibilities you will grow spiritually.

In a past life you were well disciplined and displayed leadership skills. You were a hard worker and achieved you aims with responsibility and determination. You also learnt self-discipline, how to use your will and power as well as maturity.

In transcendental astrology Saturn binds you to the earth plane so that you understand the spiritual lesson it brings. Once the lesson has been integrated and understood, Saturn frees the bonds that tie you to the past.

KARMIC HEALTH

Saturn rules the bones, teeth and skin. Saturn stays in each sign approximately two and a half years and takes an average of 29 years to complete the zodiac. Most of us will experience our first Saturn return (where Saturn was at your time of birth) between the ages of 28-30 and have no more than three Saturn transits in our lifetime.

Saturn has rulership over the feminine sign of Capricorn and is the ruler of the 10th house in the natural zodiac. Positively, Saturn signifies determination, hard work and the perseverance we need to achieve our goals. Traditionally it once ruled the masculine sign of Aquarius. If the Saturn is found in the tenth house in Druidic Soul Star Astrology, it represents a powerful and influential past life.

URANUS

Uranus can be either male or female and always symbolizes an independent person that desires personal freedom and no limitations.

Uranus was discovered in 1781. Appearing as a slight faint object, Uranus can be seen with keen eyesight on an exceptionally clear night.

In a birth chart, Uranus is the planet of independence and personal freedom and it is known as the rebel of the zodiac. Saturn always plays by the rules, but Uranus says rules are made to be broken regardless of the consequences. Uranus can show you where you dare to be different by its placement in your birth chart. Uranus is the planet of surprise, ruling all things unexpected. Uranus energy always comes out of the blue!

Uranus in a Druidic Soul Star Chart describes a past life where you were determined to have freedom of expression.

In a past life you were willing to rebel against the order or establishment and you were especially independent, eccentric and maverick. Uranus also indicates that you were once a student of the Magical Arts or the Occult. This may manifest today as an interest in metaphysics and you have inherited psychic ability.

Certainly, in that past life you loved your independence and probably stayed single always needing the freedom to truly express yourself. Thus, in this lifetime, you probably still wish to have a certain degree of freedom and hate restraint.

Uranus rules earthquakes and other natural disasters and in a past life you were probably caught up in such an event. Uranus has rulership over Aquarius and 11th house in the natural horoscope.

In transcendental astrology Uranus is the Great Awakener as it awakens the Soul to the World of Spirit. It breaks down the old patterns of karma so that you can free yourself of the old and ring in the new.

KARMIC HEALTH

Uranus rules the circulatory and involuntary nervous system.

In transcendental astrology, Uranus is the Soul Awakener who teaches us to understand one's karma and to break free of karmic restraint and grow spiritually.

NEPTUNE

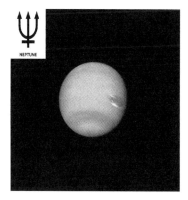

*The energy of Neptune is traditionally masculine and
therefore represents a masculine incarnation. However, use
your own intuition to interpret its gender.*

Neptune was discovered in 1846 in the outermost realms of the solar
system. In Greek Mythology Neptune was Poseidon, God of the Sea
and so Neptune rules all things related to the ocean such as boats,
fishing and marine life.

Poseidon had a shrine at the centre of Atlantis and as such often
connects an individual to an Atlantean Soul Group. However, apart
from Atlantis there may be other lost continents, islands and countries
which lie undiscovered beneath Neptune's vast oceans.

Neptune energy rules daydreaming and delights in bringing illusion.
It terms of the weather, Neptune is the mist that obscures the lay of
the land. Likewise internally, everything looks different through the
Neptunian mists of the mind.

Neptune has a deep mystical and spiritual side. It reveals that in a past
life you were a member of a spiritual group, had medium powers and
you were incredibly psychic. Millennia ago, you were a Seer of great
worth and you were noted for your sensitivity and the ability to see
through the mists of time. Your keen perception helped and inspired
others. After incarnating in Atlantis, you may have reincarnated as an
Egyptian or a Celt – a part of a spiritual group or order. However, let
your own intuition guide you with Neptune's mystical energy!

In a past life, Neptune gave you faith, insight, and the ability to see beyond the Third Dimension. However, due to the association with Atlantis Neptune may bestow a karmic fear of confined spaces or water. Neptune also rules imprisonment.

In a past life you displayed a great sense of compassion for the less fortunate. This act of human kindness raised your vibrational level and even today, you have a strong sense of equality and desire to help others who are less fortunate than yourself. Traits that have been carried over give you latent psychic power and profound mystical knowledge.

KARMIC HEALTH

As a challenging karmic force, Neptune governs dreams, trances, hypnosis, drugs, alcohol, illusion and escapism. Neptune energy can cause addictions to alcohol food and drugs as well producing physical aliments that have a psychology origin.

Neptune is the modern-day ruler of the feminine sign of Pisces, which governs the 12th house and ancient karma and secrets. If Neptune is found in the twelfth house in Druidic Soul Star Astrology, it represents a powerful and influential Atlantean past life.

In transcendental astrology Neptune represents the Higher evolved Soul that gives unconditional love to all.

PLUTO

In Greek Mythology, Pluto was Hades the God of the underworld. Pluto is the planet of rebirth, regeneration and transformation. It has been likened to the symbol of the Phoenix rising up from the fiery ashes reborn and anew. Pluto rules obstruction, decay, death and rebirth. Pluto's place in your birth chart is where you may find a constant state of turmoil and continual change and is where you realize that life goes on no matter what you must endure.

Pluto is all-powerful and knows how to push our buttons. Pluto can be an alchemic teacher that destroys aspects of our lives in order to transform us but the process may be long and painful.

Certainly, in a past life you were a powerful person. You were highly clairvoyant and could sense the vibrations of different realms and levels of consciousness. You were a leader such as a government official, a leader of the priesthood, or the figurehead of a large organisation.

You were once mentally strong and a dynamic person that was fearless, yet acted shrewdly, and was never fearful of change. You were recognised for your powerful position and may have even had the ability to heal the sick to transform people's health.

Pluto is a distant planet and as such represents a very distant past life or even an off-planet past life. Pluto rules lost kingdoms that lie beneath the soil which remain hidden from view. Pluto rules lost civilisations of the ancient world yet to be rediscovered.

Traits that have been carried over into this incarnation give you latent power and the ability to transform other peoples' lives. However, challenging Pluto past life energy can also wreak havoc and destruction. This is because Pluto governs all forms of destruction and recuperation, which include medicine and healing.

In the distant past you liked to control a situation and in this life you still like to control. However, as karma can express duality, you may attract disruptive forces or a strong Pluto type that likes to control you.

KARMIC HEALTH

Pluto rules the reproductive organs, as this is where the process of life begins. Pluto also rules puberty and sexual maturity.

No one can deny the intensity and power of Pluto energy. Pluto has rulership over Scorpio and the eighth house in the natural horoscope. If Pluto is found in this eighth house in Druidic Soul Star Astrology, it represents a powerful and influential past life.

CHIRON THE WOUNDED HEALER

Chiron orbits between the ringed planet of Saturn and Uranus. With its elliptical orbit it can cross the orbit of Saturn and touch the orbit of Uranus.

Its metaphysical symbol is a centaur, which is a creature who is half man and half horse, this symbolism mirrors and integrates its dual nature as comet and asteroid.

Its astrological glyph and influence is a 'key'. A key can open doorways and portals. The key can open inner and outer dimensions sometimes in unassuming ways such as a small key can open a large door.

Chiron is called the Wounded Healer, the Teacher of Higher Knowledge and the Bridge between the material and spiritual realms.

Chiron can be seen as a metaphysical energy which rules all of the holistic healing arts and hands on healing such as massage, polarity therapy, reflexology or spiritual healing that use the laying on of hands. Adapting to an ever-changing culture, Chiron is associated with computers and electronics, especially those methods that manipulate or compress time. This is because of it heavenly place and orbital path, as Chiron is a link between Satrun Lord of Time, which is linear and limited, and Uranian time, which is 'soul time', that is not confined by Saturn's linear time measurement. Chiron energy also rules initiation and initiatory processes.

Chiron shows that in a past life you were a healer, teacher, or a keeper of keys. Certainly, you were initiated into a Mystery School and gained access to ancient knowledge. By learning a healing skill you will reactivate this past life memory which will enhance your inherited ability to heal and to understand illness and dis-ease.

EXERCISE:
ATTUNING TO A PLANET, RECEIVING ANCIENT WISDOM
LEFT BRAIN EXERCISE

It is a good idea to study the planets and I suggest that you find your own keywords which describe their attributes. After which spend some meditative time and contemplate the planet's energy and the keywords.

IMPARTING GREAT WISDOM:
RIGHT BRAIN EXERCISE

You may wish to do the following exercise.

My approach to learning the meaning of the planets is different to other astrologers. My Druid guide told me as well as reading about the planets (left-brain activity) we can make a Sacred Connection to the living heart of the planet. You can do this by asking the planet if you can get to know its meaning and to lovingly impart its wisdom to you in servitude of humanity. Sense this request being received. If it feels right to do so, imagine or sense a light cord from your heart that reaches across time and space to the heart of the planet–or vice versa. Esoterically speaking, you are making a metaphysical connection to the planet and its timeless divinity. Now ask the planet if you can make a deep conscious connection and simply be receptive to any inflow of images, thoughts, or feelings that may come to your inner mind. Do not judge anything and allow any thoughts to come and go. Anytime you require information regarding a past life associated with a particular planet, you can 'ask' the planet to impart its truth and wisdom by following this exercise. Keep a journal of your planetary connections, images or conversations…

Chapter Four
The Astrological Houses

*T*o interpret a Druidic Soul Star chart you need to know the general meaning of the astrological houses. Druidic Soul Star astrology only uses 6 of the 12 houses which are the even house numbers: 2, 4, 6, 8, 10, and 12. Listed below are the exoteric meaning of all 12 houses and the meaning of the six Druidic Soul Star houses.

The houses show how the planetary energies,
the past lives, are expressed.

THE FIRST HOUSE AND YOUR RISING SIGN

The first house of an astrological chart has the sign that was ascending over the horizon at the moment you were born, which is known as the Rising Sign or the Ascendant.

The first house reveals the way we come across, which includes our appearance and personality. It is what makes us each so *personally* different. This house rules our personal and projected self. In medieval times, it ruled life, appearance, beauty, riches, fortune and success. It is associated with the zodiac sign of Aries.

THE SECOND HOUSE - EXOTERIC MEANING

The second house is concerned with how we respond and relate to possessions, property, material goods, income, money, and the like. The second house always refers to how we secure ourselves in the material world, the kind of response we get from life and those around us. In medieval times, it ruled profit and loss as well as mercantile matters.

DRUIDIC SOUL STAR MEANING

This placement shows past life responses to the materialistic side of life which include past experiences dealing with property, money, wealth and possessions. For instance, if Saturn (planet of limitation) was in

this house it would indicate financial limitations in a past life, perhaps even poverty. Whereas, Jupiter (planet of expansion and positive karma) would show that there was abundance and material wealth. However, the deeper meaning of this house is Self Love and Spiritual Growth. Self Love is about learning to love yourself, the Kingdoms of Nature and sharing your love and material resources with those around you. It is about letting go of any poverty or material issues, becoming receptive to love, and allowing abundance into your life.

The second house teaches us spiritual values which cannot be found in the material realm. On a higher level, it is about serving and helping those whose consciousness is in embedded in matter, to live in harmony with the spiritual as well as the material planes of existence.

This house aligns the personality with nature spirits and spirit guides. It can indicate the querent is a Spiritual Teacher. It is associated with the zodiac sign of Taurus.

KEYWORDS

Learning the lesson of money, poverty or riches. A way of harmonising any financial spiritual debts. Spiritual values, Self Love and karmic resources.

THE THIRD HOUSE - EXOTERIC MEANING

The third house rules connections, communications such as wires, tubes as well as the mind, the voice-the spoken word and all forms of writing. It also rules explorations, investigations and inquiry and research of all kinds. It is through the energy of the third house that we explore and search for answers and understanding. This is a very *mental* house, concerned with finding, furthering, researching, and questioning. Traditionally it rules short journeys, siblings. In medieval times, it ruled all relatives, letters and short journeys. It is associated with the zodiac sign of Gemini.

THE FOURTH HOUSE IN EXOTERIC ASTROLOGY

The fourth house is where we set down our roots, find our limits, and generally secure ourselves. In the energy of the fourth house, we seek and make a home and the base from which we can work, feel and experience. This is the root of our experience, the core of who we are. It represents the Mother and the Soul.

In medieval times, it ruled parents, property, treasures, agriculture and mines.

DRUIDIC SOUL STAR MEANING

The Fourth House reveals past lives associated with your family's karmic history, Soul groups, karmic links to your parents, children and sometimes the land upon which you live.

Before your birth, your soul chose the souls who were going to be your parents, the religion by which you would live. Selected the village, town or city where you would be raised and chose the experiences, or soul lessons, that would allow you to evolve spiritually.

For millennia, this astrological house has symbolised endings and can describe the karmic circumstances you may face during the latter years of your life. The Moon in this location would indicate a karmic link to the Mother and the Sun or Saturn a karmic link to your father or a male in this incarnation. It is associated with the zodiac sign of Cancer.

KEYWORDS

Past lives and karma associated with the parents, family members and children Your karmic foundation. The latter years of your life.

THE FIFTH HOUSE - IN EXOTERIC ASTROLOGY

The fifth house has to do with awareness, self-confidence, the emotions and its expression. Here there is always a growing sense of self-confidence and even a pride of self or ownership. All forms of expression and offspring are connected to this house, such as romances, children, animals, creative expression, and so on.

In medieval times, it ruled women, luxury, eating, drinking, pleasure, and servants It is associated with the zodiac sign of Leo.

THE SIXTH HOUSE - IN EXOTERIC ASTROLOGY

The sixth house is associated with the zodiac sign of Virgo which is depicted in the heavens as a goddess holding an ear of wheat.

The Sixth house rules health, nutrition and hygiene as well as jobs, personal service and employees.

In medieval times, it ruled diseases, servants, misfortune and domestic animals.

DRUIDIC SOUL STAR MEANING

The sixth house within the upward heaven-ascending triangle governs karmic health. We read earlier that each planet is associated with a particular part of the body and if there is a karmic health issue, the associated area may manifest an aliment.

The sixth house also represents servitude to humankind. It often indicates that in a past life you were a healer or in some way a helper.

When we intuitively interpret the Druidic Soul Star chart, we sense the right expression of the past life and the gender of the planet can guide us further. For instance, the Moon's placement here would suggest that in a past life you were a female healer, or you at the very least cared for other people in a motherly and loving way.

The Karmic lesson of the sixth house is to be of service to others as humanity is a family. We are all the same only our stories are different. Animals or pets that are close to us can be karmically linked through the celestial energy of the sixth house.

KEYWORDS

Health issues, karmic link to animals or pets and service.

THE SEVENTH HOUSE - IN EXOTERIC ASTROLOGY

The seventh house is the house of partnerships, marriage, relationships and your social life. The energy of the seventh house takes our personal self into an awareness of other people, community and the like. This includes spiritual awakening and the discovery that we are more than just our personality. It rules friends and enemies. In medieval times, it ruled marriage, prostitutes, thieves, robbers and dishonours.

THE EIGHTH HOUSE - IN EXOTERIC ASTROLOGY

The eighth house traditionally rules sex, death and rebirth. It rules other people's resources and it has a depth of quality.

In medieval times, it ruled death, legacies, trouble, suffering and poverty.

DRUIDIC SOUL STAR MEANING

The eighth house is an important sector in the Earth Star triangle. Traditionally, this house focuses on death, the afterlife and rebirth. Therefore, it connects the past, present to the future. Also, it represents an interest in the occult as well as psychology.

Planets in this house always indicate that you have been active in a spiritual or psychic way. You learnt the occult arts and have inherited psychic potential from past lives.

Planets in the eighth house also can describe past life experiences where you have either honourably shared, or selfishly used other people's resources, such as material possessions, marital finances, property and legacies. Often described as a testing-ground for future karmic gains, this house reveals deep buried emotions and past debts.

Certain planets in this sector verify the circumstances surrounding the death of a previous incarnation, especially if karmic shock-trauma occurred. For example, Mars in this house may indicate that in a previous life one died in a battle or war situation and Uranus a sudden death.

KEYWORDS

Inherited karmic debts or rewards. Spiritual and occult knowledge and deep buried emotions.

THE NINTH HOUSE - IN EXOTERIC ASTROLOGY

The ninth house governs higher education, the in-laws, long journeys and religion. Also, essential ideas, philosophy, and the knowledge that makes us grow. In medieval times it ruled religious matters, long journeys and dreams. It also rules publishing, television, radio and electronic media.

THE TENTH HOUSE - IN EXOTERIC ASTROLOGY

The tenth house rules one's public image, reputation, career and the parents, usually the father, and it is the house of practical vision and clairvoyance. In medieval times, it ruled fortune, honours, kings, glory, fame and victory.

DRUIDIC SOUL STAR MEANING

The tenth house is the highest part of the Druidic Soul Star chart representing a connection to the heavens above. At the time of your birth, any planet in this sector was high in the sky above the place where you were born and it activated your crown chakra. A sacred in pouring of celestial knowledge occurred which resides deep within your soul. This is the House of the old soul, the initiate, the teacher, and the wisdom keeper. It is a sacred placement.

Planets in this house impart a gift or a blessing and do not express their negative shadow as the light of this house dispels all darkness so that the knowledge within the Soul can express itself and impart its truth to humanity.

You have a true purpose and innate leadership skills. Tapping into the deep awareness imparted to you at birth can be achieved through meditation or an esoteric art such as automatic writing or channelling. You are a giver and you have much to give.

This house is traditionally ruled by Capricorn personified as the mountain goat that climbs to the top of the mountain and has a vision – planets herein represent a past life where you studied and excelled at a subject. Within you is the visionary, the prophet and the healer.

KEYWORDS

Old soul. Karmic gifts or talent. A blessing, leadership skills, prophet.

THE ELEVENTH HOUSE - IN EXOTERIC ASTROLOGY

The eleventh house encourages our visions and dreams to work. It rules associates and friends as well as ideals, social values and aspirations. This house has always been connected with altruistic and humanitarian goals and trying to set them in motion. It is the house of friends and the community of 'brotherhood and sisterhood'.

In medical times, it ruled protection, presents, friends, riches joy, hope and confidence.

THE TWELFTH HOUSE - IN EXOTERIC ASTROLOGY

The twelfth house bestows the energy to turn our dreams into reality. However, this house also covers what we are willing to put up with, and the sacrifices we will make, in order to manifest what is really important.

The twelfth house is associated to prisons, institutions, betrayal and self-undoing. It rules karma and all things that are hidden and secrets.

In medieval times it ruled loss, imprisonment, secret enemies, vagabonds, beggars and misfortune.

DRUIDIC SOUL STAR MEANING

The twelfth house rules distant and ancient karma. Planets herein are significant as they often portray a past life bound by karma. It is the house that rules Soul Contracts that which binds us to the past and to the law of cause and effect. However, once the karma is understood, forgiven and released, it can set us free to dream our dreams awake.

This house rules prisons, institutions, betrayals and working behind the scenes. It can rule karmic fears such as confined spaces, water and heights.

It can represent a past life that was spent learning the occult arts often associated with the ancient temples of Atlantis, Lemuria or Egypt.

Planets in this house often give us the desire to retreat from society to explore the inner spiritual realms. As this is the last house in the order of the zodiac, it ensures a new cycle, a new day and a new chapter. Quite often, this house is associated with lost civilisations, ancient and esoteric rites and humankind's most distant past.

KEYWORDS

Deep rooted and ancient karma, and karmic fears. Psychic ability. Working behind the scenes. Metaphysical and occult knowledge.

EXERCISE:
ATTUNING TO THE ENERGIES OF THE HOUSE
LEFT BRAIN EXERCISE

It is a good idea to study the house and choose your *own* keywords to describe them. After which spend some meditative time and contemplate the house's energy and the keywords.

MY DRUID GUIDE IMPARTING GREAT WISDOM

Ask the house – which is a living area of the solar system called the ecliptic belt which contains the zodiacal constellations –if you can get to know its meaning and to lovingly impart its wisdom to you in servitude of humanity. We can make a Sacred Connection to the house by attuning to the stars of the zodiac. For the Second House attune to the stars of Taurus, by visualising the stars in your Mind's Eye, for the Fourth House the stars of Cancer, the Sixth Virgo, the Eighth Scorpio, Tenth Capricorn and the Twelfth Pisces.

Esoterically speaking, you are making a metaphysical connection to the zodiac and its timeless divinity. You are asking the zodiac to make a deep connection.

Chapter Five
Putting It All Together

*I*nterpretation of a Soul Star chart is quite straightforward. You need to take the attributes of the planet alongside the keywords of the house and blend them together. Later, we will explore the interpretations in detail. Below is a list of tips for interpretation.

TIPS FOR INTERPRETATION

•Always use your intuition: listen to your inner voice for guidance. If you know the gender of the person, for example, Venus as a woman, try to attune to the past life by asking:what was the colour of the hair, eyes and *sense* the information.

•Ask the planet to assist you: make spiritual contact with the planet, ask in a loving manner for guidance.

•The house placement shows how the karma was played out. For instance, a planet in the forth house implies karma related to the home and family. Ask the house to assist you by making spiritual contact with the zodiac.

•If you get any information, intuitive guidance or you sense anything always thank the planetary body and the zodiac.

•I have learnt to trust the energy of the planets and the zodiac. My readings have been compared to information gleaned from past life regression therapy sessions; both were very similar. Accurate readings are the result of using standard astrological symbolism as described in this book and intuition. Druidic Soul Star will open your energy field to the stars as long as you come from a caring place of servitude.

•Retrograde motion: read the positive as well as the retrograde motion interpretation for a holistic understanding of the planetary energy.

•For the future: for a broader understanding, you may wish to learn what the planet's placement in a particular sign means. It is not fully necessary for Druidic Soul Star astrology but it could help. Apply this as an additional tool *after* you have become familiar with the planets in the houses. I have a Druid Soul Star

Level 1 course and I am compiling a Level II Druidic Soul Star course with EsotericCollege.com which will include zodiac sign placements, aspects and transits – discovering how the karmic past can be triggered.

CHART INTERPRETATION

Let us take another look at Leeann's chart. Each planet within the chart represents a past life that embodies certain characteristics. I always look at all of the planets in the Druidic Soul Star chart and then I see which one draws my attention, or which planet I am attracted to, and I begin with interpreting that planet. I just use my intuition to guide me.

The Moon in the 12th house attracted my attention, so I would start the reading by interpreting the energies associated with this planet and house placement. Here is an example which outlines the attributes associated with the client's past lives giving a description of who they were.

LEEANN: A DRUIDIC SOUL STAR INTERPRETATION

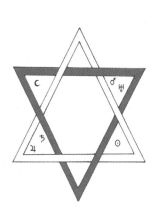

The Moon shows me that you have karmic ties with your mother or a close female relative such as your daughter. You were all once a part of a Soul Group that incarnated together millennia ago as the 12th house represents ancient karma. You have all been together before as far back as Atlantis.

In this past life you were a female who was trained as a psychic or medium with great sensitivity that was probably a part of an ancient temple complex.

This house rules karmic fears of confined spaces – imprisonment, water and heights. It also represents someone who has learnt the occult arts and has been exceptionally psychic in the past, perhaps in the ancient temples of Atlantis, Lemuria or Egypt.

Blending the information of the planet's attributes, the meaning of the house, and attuning to the chart, is a great way of sensing past lives and bringing the chart to life.

Sun in the Sixth house: In another incarnation, but this time as a man, you cared for, and deeply respected, other people, and now you have a karmic blessing for those actions. You were faithful and loyal to those you loved and you have inherited these traits. I feel that you may have held a position of authority and exercised leadership skills but with servitude and fairness.

As well as having a karmic link to certain females of your family, as described earlier by the Moon's sacred placement, another karmic family link is evident. The sun suggests a deep karmic connection to a male family member such as your father, son, brother or grandfather.

In a past life, you may have been a healer that took exceptional care in your work. Undoubtedly, you have inherited the gift of healing as the sixth house rules health and well-being. The placement of the sun and moon give you psychic ability and the gift of healing.

Mars in the eighth house: Mars in this position represents a past life as a strong and courageous man who may have been involved in a battle or a war of sorts. *I would ask if the querent has any birthmarks or reddish patches on the body. These may be the residue of wounds from a past life battle.* Mars rules the head, blood and muscles and so if you had endured a head injury during this past life you may suffer from migraines. Any past burns or inflammation, may have left a birthmark on your body. *Mars rules fevers and so I would ask if the client suffers from high temperatures when coming down with a cold?*

I would use the scanning method which is described later to see if there is any psychic residue influencing the querent in this life.

I would ask if Leeann has a strong bold nature now – sometimes karma plays out the opposite way. So she may be shy or reserved.

Uranus in the eighth house: Uranus energy is often a male and shows that in a past life you once had a rebellious nature and you loved to travel and experience new things. Possibly now you are often restless and do not like routine. Uranus also indicates that you were once a student of the Magical Arts or the Occult. This may manifest today as an interest in metaphysics and you have inherited psychic ability. Certainly, in that past life you loved your independence and probably stayed single, always needing the freedom to truly express yourself. Thus, in this lifetime, you probably still wish to have a certain degree of freedom, even in relationships and you hate restraint.

Uranus rules earthquakes and other natural disasters and you may have been caught up in such an event. Situated in the house of Death may imply a sudden death?

Jupiter in the Second House: The energy of the Jupiter is traditionally masculine and therefore represents a male incarnation. Jupiter brings karmic rewards and good things to the house it occupies in your Druidic Soul Star chart.

Jupiter bestows good fortune, as karmically you have deserved it. This is because in a previous life you were a wise and generous soul who shared your material wealth with others. You were helpful and came to the assistance of others. Many times you displayed acts of selflessness.

You had a strong spiritual faith and may have been in the priesthood, an astronomer or a philosopher. You have inherited a strong sense of justice and so in this life you hate injustice and despise unfairness.

Saturn in the second house: Saturn energy tends to be male. Certainly, its placement in your chart shows that in one past life you met and faced your karmic responsibilities.

Saturn in a Druidic Soul Star chart signifies karmic duty and that you are an old Soul. Saturn shows that by excepting your responsibilities you will grow spiritually. In a past life, you were well disciplined and displayed leadership skills. You were a hard worker and achieved you aims with responsibility and determination. You also learnt self-discipline, how to use your will and power as well as maturity.

It seems that the lesson of money, material possessions was important for your soul development as two planets are in the Second House emphasising this karmic lesson. In one life represented by Jupiter, you had wealth and then in another past life represented by Saturn you experienced poverty.

So I would ask the client if their money situation fluctuates, or do they sometimes find themselves juggling money. On the other hand, perhaps these two opposite past lives forged a karmic path leading to financial balance between the spiritual and material realms.

Chapter Six
Understanding The Earth Star Triangle

Standard interpretations for houses four, eight and twelve

The earth star triangle consists of the water triplicate of Cancer (house 4), Scorpio (house 8) and Pisces (house 12). Esoterically speaking, the water signs symbolise the need to overcome the astral realms of desire, negative emotions and fear. Indeed, some members of the Victorian Mystery Schools thought that water symbolised 'Time' and thus Karma.

The downward triangle teaches us about our emotions, such as emotional control or desire. If emotional lessons have been ignored, misused, or not fully understood, they are re-enacted through our emotions and manifest in each incarnation until the spiritual lesson is understood or resolved. Emotional lessons and tests are usually played out in our family, or personal relationships, and they can be painful or they can bring great joy and wisdom. Once the emotional test is understood the doorway is open to experience emotional freedom, unconditional love, harmony and peace.

From Transcendental Astrology by A.G.S. Norris

'The advanced spiritual lesson of peace is often difficult on the earth plane; however, the Soul needs to learn peace to return to the higher planes and it must learn to find love and God within'.

EARTH WATER-BODY WATER

Water has memory and its elemental role is unique. It is my belief that our body water holds onto memories as well as the mind. I have developed a healing system that unites our physical, emotional and mental bodies with the Earth's sacred inner waters. These deep and pure waters can cleanse and purify our body water and also release past life or current life tensions. For more information, please go to

EsotericCollege.com or theaveburyexperience.co.uk

TRANSCENDENTAL ASTROLOGY – DRUIDIC SOUL STAR HOUSES

According to transcendental astrologers, before one becomes a 'perfect human being', peace of Body, Soul and of Mind must be attained. We find first contact with the Water signs through the sign of the Soul, Cancer. Cancer is the portal to Peace. Cancer teaches us to release fear, negative emotions, to nurture, and to help others. When we help others, the Spiritual Family of Humanity breathes and expands. The stars of Cancer and the Fourth House teach that the Astral or Desire body is at the seat of these emotions, and should be controlled by the Mind and Body, through the power of Love. Cancer has the potential to be the Prophet of Peace. The Spiritual Rays of Cancer teach us to master self-control, release fear and to know when peace is obtained it can transform life.

The Spiritual Rays of Scorpio teach spiritual understanding of the mysteries of life. Sex, death and rebirth are the cycle of life and within the rebirth of one's Soul there can be an in-depth understanding that the Soul's unconditional love can create a pathway to harmony and peace. The Soul is regenerated by the Power of Unconditional Love, and it seeks Eternal Peace and Union with the Divine, which is found in the last sign of the zodiac, Pisces.

The Spiritual Rays of Pisces bring peace and harmony that can be shared with others and humanity. The two fishes are no longer swimming in opposite directions as their zodiacal glyph represents, but have found peace and harmony in the waters of life and now swim side by side towards the light of the Godhead. The Union of the Soul with the Divine is the true purpose of life symbolised by the alchemists that transmuted base lead, which is the fear and desire of human nature into Alchemic Spiritual Gold.

The sacred teachings of the water signs have revealed their zodiacal message that true peace cannot be found in the emotions (Cancer) or the physical body, sex (Scorpio) and through Pisces we learn to bring sustenance from the spiritual plane to Earth and to be reunited with the Divine.

TRUST YOUR INTUITION

It was said earlier that the best way to interpret a Druidic Soul Star chart is to use your own intuition and blend the meaning of the house and the planet. Remain mindful that what I would say may be different to what you would say, as your Soul understanding of life may be different. We may both see different elements within a chart but each interpretation would be relevant. Druidic Soul Star interpretation asks for you to be intuitive and to trust your Soul to read the past life experiences of another Soul.

However, I have included a basic interpretation guide of each of the planets in the Druidic Soul Star houses to act only as a guide, and certainly *not* the only interpretation. Let your interpretation come from the heart which will be far better than from a book. We are all connected and there is no separation and Druidic Soul Star connects heaven to earth.

BRINGING DEEP AWARENESS

A Druidic Soul Star reading can bring a deep awareness and a profound insight into the invisible undercurrents that silently influence our daily lives. Trust your intuition as to where in the chart you should begin your reading – go by which area of the chart you feel drawn to. Each planet within the Earth Star triangle represents a past life that embodies certain characteristics.

Using descriptive planetary symbolism translated thousands of years ago by ancient astronomer-priests, an overall impression of the past life can be identified.

PLANETS IN THE FOURTH HOUSE
THE FIRST STEP TOWARDS KARMIC AWARENESS

As I stated earlier, begin your reading by looking at the chart and sensing where you should begin or by which planet draws your attention. However, if you are unsure or not particularly drawn to a planet, the fourth house is a good starting point as it symbolises the Soul.

The fourth house is an important sector of a Druidic Soul Star chart, because as we saw earlier, it represents the spiritual stem of the lotus flower. In the womb of the Cancer and the fourth house, a Spiritual Stem is born that leads to enlightenment. Resolving karma in this sector allows significant blockages to be removed, so that the stem can grow stalwart and strong.

The fourth house reveals your karmic past associated with your family, Soul groups, your children and sometimes the land upon which you live. Before your birth, your soul chose the souls who were going to be your parents, the religion by which you would live. Selected the village, town or city where you would be raised and chose the experiences or soul lesson's that would allow you to evolve spiritually.

For millennia, this astrological house has symbolised endings and can describe the circumstances you may face during the latter years of your life and the way in which events in your previous incarnation ended.

THE SUN IN THE FOURTH HOUSE
MALE INCARNATION

The Sun often bestows a spiritual blessing

The Sun in the fourth house brings a spiritual blessing indicating deep emotional ties between family members, especially the father. In a woman's chart, it reveals a karmic bond with a partner, husband, brother or son. You are all a part of a soul group or soul family and have incarnated together before.

In fact, the influence of one or both of your parents is strong for good or for bad. If you have a challenging relationship with your parents, partner or children, there is deep-rooted karma that needs resolving. Forgiveness is always the first step towards letting go of karmic residue. The Sun in this position is all-healing, as it can cleanse and release any negative karma associated with the Earth Star triangle. Later, we will explore some healing techniques which help release past life issues.

Provided you stay on a positive karmic path, beneficial influences will be given to you and your children.

Inherited from a previous incarnation you have a compelling need to establish a secure home, to put down roots and provide a safe environment for your family. You have a strong sense of family loyalty and karmic development is influenced by family relationships and attitudes; by being supportive, caring and nurturing spiritual progress is assured. At times, when life becomes difficult you may have the wish to retreat from society into the safety of your home.

Traditionally, the Sun in this position indicates that the first part of this life may prove challenging with prosperity and domestic security occurring towards the latter years.

THE MOON IN THE FOURTH HOUSE
FEMALE INCARNATION

The Moon in the fourth house exerts a powerful influence because astrologically this house is ruled by the Moon that corresponds to the sign of Cancer.

In one past life, deep emotional bonds between you and your family were forged. You have inherited psychic ability from a female relative, possibly your grandmother, aunt, mother or sister. Alternatively your daughter has inherited a psychic gift.

In a man's chart, it reveals a karmic bond with a female relative, partner, wife or daughter.

This lunar placement can be challenging, as it suggests a tendency to become too dependent upon the family. Consequently, independence and self-reliance will accelerate personal and spiritual growth.

Security is very important to you and the types of things that you collect may serve as reminders of your past lives. Many changes of residence can occur until you find your personal foundation or roots and find your spiritual home – the land upon which you resonate. Yet, the Moon's calming karmic rays indicate that the home will provide a secure environment for spiritual growth. You have inherited strong psychic ability and a deep respect for nature. In a previous life, you communicated with the elemental kingdoms, and by reconnecting with nature, your psychic sensitivity will unfold. You may have inherited from previous lives interests in gardening, real estate, cookery or holistic subjects.

You have a karmic advantage as the Moon's placement gives you an intuitive understanding of your karmic past so be guided by your own sensitive nature.

MERCURY IN THE FOURTH HOUSE
MALE INCARNATION

In a recent past life you lived a nomadic life style or you constantly travelled and moved around. You had a great sense of adventure and wanderlust and you were exceptionally curious always wanting to experience new ideas, people and places.

This strong karmic memory may be subtly influencing your personality traits in this life. If so, you have probably changed residences frequently or enjoy travelling. Certainly, you feel frustrated by personal confinement, become easily bored and dislike repetitive routine. The Soul Lesson is to balance the desire for movement and freedom with the need to create domestic security. Achieving this equilibrium will allow the past to be integrated into the present.

You were studious, with literary interests, which is a trait that you have also inherited. You still like to study at home.

There is also a strong karmic connection to a brother or sister.

MERCURY RETROGRADE MOTION

In a recent past life, you repeatedly changed residences and found it difficult to settle in one place. A Karmic lesson is to settle down and to make a home. In addition, misunderstandings between family members probably involving a brother, sister or cousin caused anxiety problems. Mental biases were carried forward into this incarnation which may be unconsciously projected upon certain family members. If so, the cycle of friction should be resolved and healed. We will explore healing techniques later.

You have inherited intellectual skills and your home may be used for work, or you could pursue a hobby which could be turned into a career. You have inherited karmic interests in ecology, earth sciences, reading and writing.

VENUS IN THE FOURTH HOUSE
FEMALE INCARNATION

In a previous incarnation, family relationships were harmonious and you were emotionally close to your family and friends. Karma is intimately connected to the emotional needs of your family. Certainly, you have strong karmic ties with your children, one of whom will have an artistic gift or a creative talent.

In this past life, you worked the land and were involved in agriculture. Today, your innate love of nature is expressed through gardening, cookery or a deep love of your homeland. Your home is especially important to you and no doubt artistically decorated as you have a natural flair for creating beauty within your surroundings.

You have inherited an artistic nature with a gift of making people welcome in your home.

In a previous life you overcame material greed and avarice. Karmic recognition will give material comfort and security during this incarnation if the former karmic attitude is retained. Material benefits and inheritances are often associated with this placement, which if unselfishly shared will help promote spiritual growth.

The latter part of this incarnation may be especially pleasant and comfortable as this is your karmic reward for helping others in the past – by inviting them into the safety of your home.

The ancient Egyptians and the Druids are associated with the zodiac sign of Taurus which Venus rules.

VENUS RETROGRADE MOTION

In a previous incarnation your home life may have been disruptive or challenging. Emotional attention may have been directed towards other family members leaving you feeling lonely, isolated or jealous. If psychic residue persists, similar emotional responses or circumstances will surface during this incarnation. For instance, a partner may place their job and material gains before the emotional needs of you and your family. Alternatively, you may attract a partner that makes you feel second best. By embracing, talking and working such issues through, any karmic residue will dissipate and a productive phase will emerge.

In a past life you were artistic and have inherited a creative talent which will develop with maturity. Towards the latter years, you may acquire wealth or property and live comfortably.

MARS IN THE FOURTH HOUSE
MALE INCARNATION

Mars in the fourth house is challenging indicating testing karmic ties between family members. During a recent past life high emotions, such as anger and jealously, caused persistent disagreements creating an intense home environment. There was a constant battle of wills between family members, some of whom were domineering and overpowering. Periodically, karmic energy may resurface and silently trigger family conflicts or irrational irritability projected towards family members. This placement identifies the need to bring peace and harmony to family life as a necessary step towards spiritual growth and to resolve age-old karma.

In a man's chart, there is a karmic link with a male relative. Likewise, in a woman's chart there is a powerful karmic connection with a male relative, partner, male friend, son or husband.

In the latter years of this incarnation, you will acquire property, land or buildings. This placement gives a strong constitution until old age.

The ancient Jewish and Muslim peoples are associated with the zodiacal sign of Aries which Mars rules.

MARS RETROGRADE MOTION

You have inherited a powerful will and therefore you are capable of transforming any aspect of your life – this is your karmic gift. You are protective towards loved ones and karma is centred on your family focussing on male members; the father, husband, brother or son etc. The energy of Mars is urging you to achieve domestic harmony and to resolve family disputes or issues.

No matter how frustrating or painful the problems; remain mindful that when the powerful and courageous energy of Mars is harnessed it can move mountains.

JUPITER IN THE FOURTH HOUSE
MALE OR FEMALE INCARNATION

Jupiter always indicates beneficial influences and karmic rewards which have culminated over many lives.

In a previous incarnation, you were exceptionally compassionate and understanding of other people's feelings and you were always willing to help those less fortunate than yourself. You retain these traits and Jupiter returns beneficial karma by providing domestic security or educational advantages.

You travelled extensively and lived in a foreign country and inner karmic memories may encourage you to rediscover the place where centuries ago you lived happily.

Spiritual and karmic benefits will come within the locality of the birthplace. Today, the home may be a centre for religious, social, philosophical or educational activities. If during your early years you shouldered family responsibilities, this placement portends good fortune towards the second half of life.

JUPITER RETROGRADES MOTION

In a past life, you shouldered domestic responsibilities and financial burdens caused by family misfortune. Consequently, in this incarnation you strive for financial solvency and domestic security. However, there is often the temptation to overspend and indulge in expensive items to beautify your surroundings, a way of trying to heal the memories of the past. Your karmic lesson is to understand that you have helped people in the past but need to know when to except help yourself.

You have inherited a deep philosophical nature and you are always willing to help others. You welcome people into your home and have a warm and inviting nature. Towards the latter years, you will live in comfort for the trials and tribulations of former years and previous lives.

It is worth noting that living aboard or experiencing different cultures will encourage personal and spiritual development.

SATURN IN THE FOURTH HOUSE
MALE INCARNATION

Saturn's placement in a chart reveals an individual's karmic responsibilities.

In the fourth house, Saturn is especially challenging indicating profound spiritual responsibilities relating to the home and family. However, you are well equipped to gain karmic progress by accepting your circumstances and you have the strength and persistence to overcome barriers and fulfil your karmic obligations.

During one past life, you constantly struggled to provide for your family and the trace memory may cause feelings of inadequacy to surface. Remain mindful that your inner strength and resourcefulness can reshape your future and redirect the karmic energy to your advantage.

Saturn's energy reveals that you once worked the land, or that you were employed in domestic service. Today professional activity may be centred on housing, real estate, or domestic issues.

The ancient Hindus people are associated with the zodiacal sign of Capricorn which Saturn rules.

SATURN RETROGRADE MOTION

Bringing karmic issues to the surface, Saturn's retrograde motion indicates family responsibilities may be placed upon you that restrict your movement and freedom. Facing your karmic responsibilities is your spiritual lesson which will ensure spiritual growth; although this area of your life may seem periodically testing, other areas of your life will bring much pleasure and happiness. This planetary placement is often associated with individuals who mature and age late in life.

URANUS IN THE FOURTH HOUSE
MALE OR FEMALE INCARNATION

Uranus in the fourth house indicates that during one past life you lived a bohemian life style, or you had an unusual family or home life. Frequent changes of residence were caused by sudden changes, and in this incarnation, there may be the irresistible urge to suddenly uproot and move on. You will be attracted to homes that display unusual architecture, or seek an alternative lifestyle.

During this former life, you were at odds with your family, social, or cultural background. For instance, you may have been a reformer, revolutionist or someone who desired social justice, equality and radical reform. This past life experience portends that you now strive for personal independence, liberation and freedom. You dislike constraint and seek to broaden your understanding by experiencing new ideologies, people and places. You like to come and go as you please!

There are strong karmic ties to close friends who at one stage in your karmic journey were close family members.

URANUS RETROGRADE MOTION

In a past life you experienced domestic upheavals, problems and upsets. You may have lost your home and possessions. Retrograde Uranus holds onto karmic energy and suddenly releases it when least expected. Therefore, domestic upsets and sudden upheavals could occur creating domestic arguments or family problems. Progressive spiritual growth requires family cooperation, reliance and trust which will ensure a more settled domestic lifestyle and future happiness. Look for the areas of family life that are challenging and you will discover hidden karmic lessons. Addressing these issues will release psychic residue initiating a natural healing process.

Friends feature strongly in your life and are accepted as family members. Your home may be used as a meeting place for group activities or spiritual development. One of your relatives had an unusual talent which you have inherited.

NEPTUNE IN THE FOURTH HOUSE
FEMALE INCARNATION

Those with Neptune in the fourth house were associated with maritime trade or lived close to water. For generations your family has developed outstanding psychic or mediumship skills and maintained strong emotional ties. You have incarnated many times together. Your natural psychic ability was developed millennia ago during the early civilisations of Sumer in ancient Mesopotamia, or Egypt in the Middle East.

Psychic or priestly families were renown throughout the ancient world. For instance, in Eleusis, Greece, the family of the Eumolpidai claimed descent from a mythical ancestor, the Son of Neptune. Guardians of holy objects the family led ceremonial processions from Athens to Eleusis and were dedicated to one another. Thus, your strong psychic lineage undoubtedly influences this incarnation and you probably have interests in the mysteries of life, holistic healing and esoteric subjects.

Certain family members are psychic and you have well-developed intuition. Significantly, over many lives, you have developed a profound understanding of nature, and as a young child you may have interacted with the devic, or angelic realms, or seen images of the past and intuitively sensed the future. Your karmic gift is your sensitive and psychic nature.

Intriguingly, Neptune's location suggests a family secret or mystery has remained untold or unresolved for generations.

NEPTUNE RETROGRADE MOTION

Neptune retrograde indicates that during one past life you experienced confused family relationships and an unstable home life. These traits may resurface as a karmic lesson and unconsciously influence your current domestic situation manifesting as a disorderly home or persistent disagreements between family members. Simply put, you may not understand each other. Domestic organization and cooperation will encourage karmic residue to dissipate and harmonious family relations to develop.

You once worked and lived by a large river or by the sea and may desire to do so again. You had deep and intuitive feelings for the land and all of nature and have inherited these qualities. Exceptional psychic ability will unfold towards your latter years and your children will inherit this gift.

PLUTO IN THE FOURTH HOUSE
MALE INCARNATION

This placement can be problematic. During one past life, a parent or relative was overtly strict or domineering and you experienced intense power struggles between family members. Karmic energy may resurface as an overbearing attitude that can be confrontational and distance family members. In adulthood, karmic residue may unconsciously attract a dictatorial partner. If this is a current issue, it is important that you heal the karmic experience by acknowledging the karmic energy and then asking for it to be let go... The Universe always supports spiritual growth and you have inherited a deep resourcefulness that can regenerate and transform any adverse situation. You can be like the Phoenix – rising from the ashes born anew.

In a previous life you developed an intense bond with nature and understood some of its most profound secrets. You were an active member of an esoteric organization such as a Magician within a mystery school, Druid, White Witch or Priest/ess etc. You are a natural dowser and geomancer and are able to communicate with the hidden beings of nature. You may also have interests in ecology and sustainable living.

PLUTO RETROGRADE MOTION

An extreme past life experience of homelessness and abandonment has left a deep emotional fear of being alone. You now strive for domestic control – which is understandable – as you unconsciously fear that you will loose your possessions 'again'. Your karmic lesson is to allow yourself to flow with the cycles of life and to trust rather than trying to manipulate situations will naturally release karmic residue.

Tune into your Spiritual Self, as you were once a Master of the Esoteric Arts. You are a natural geomancer and have the ability to relate and interact with the subtle forces of nature, such as the earth elementals, ley lines and earth energies. You can develop your spiritual nature by attuning to the higher forces of nature that are willing to assist you.

CHIRON IN THE FOURTH HOUSE

In a past life you were sensitive to the suffering of humanity, and in this life you have been gifted with the potential for being an excellent counsellor.

Chiron calls for you to know that healing comes through connecting with your emotional roots. There may be psychic residue from a past life or your Soul Family group that requires healing. Or you may need to heal your deepest roots to discover who you are. You have inherited an intense, deep and brooding nature, and you are sometimes nervous or restless.

CHIRON IN THE FOURTH HOUSE
RETROGRADE MOTION. MALE INCARNATION

In a past life you suffered during your early years, felt rejected or misunderstood. Past life childhood trauma may silently influence your current family life. Healing occurs when you look at your own childhood and heal the past by simply acknowledging and letting go. You can step into a new karmic future.

Allow the past to be released and this will free you of past pain and allow you to create the loving family you deserve. Love yourself more.

On an esoteric level, you can heal the land and assist Mother Nature to restore balance to the Earth Plane.

Chapter Seven
The Eighth House - Understanding The Past

The eighth house is an important sector in the Earth Star triangle as it is one of the petals of the flowering lotus. Traditionally, this house focuses on death, the afterlife and rebirth. Therefore, it connects the past, present and the future.

Planets in this house indicate that you have been active in a spiritual or psychic way. This may have been as part of the priesthood, or a member of a mystery school as far back as ancient Egypt. You learnt the occult arts and have inherited psychic potential from past lives.

Planets in the eighth house can describe in detail past life experiences where you have either honourably shared, or selfishly used other people's resources, such as material possessions, marital finances, property and legacies. Often described as a testing-ground for future karmic gains, this house reveals deep buried emotions and past debts .

Planets in this sector can often verify the circumstances surrounding the death of a previous incarnation, especially if karmic shock-trauma occurred. Often birthmarks identify specific areas of the physical body that were affected by the trauma. Healing the karmic aliment with spiritual light and empathy will restore physical, emotional, mental and spiritual equilibrium and resolve the karmic affliction. Healing techniques will be explored later.

SUN IN THE EIGHTH HOUSE
MALE INCARNATION

The Sun in this sector gives a karmic blessing and spiritual protection. Over several past lives you studied the psychic arts and reached a high level of spiritual awareness. Thus, in this lifetime, you were born with psychic sensitivity and an innate belief in life after death.

During childhood your clairvoyant sensitivity may not have been recognised, or easily understood by others. However, at some stage in your life, a profound spiritual experience or encounter will open the Third Eye chakra and your psychic nature will naturally develop.

With your spirit guides by your side, and your inherited wisdom subtly influencing and expanding your consciousness you are ready to embark upon a spiritual journey. You were once a healer or shaman and have inherited this gift enabling you to channel energy from one dimension to another. Silently, you are being guided by the inner light and consciousness of the divine central Sun.

You are an old soul whose prophetic insight can foresee future cycles. Use your sensitivity to help others and for the greater good of humankind.

MOON IN THE EIGHTH HOUSE
FEMALE INCARNATION

Regardless of your current gender, you were a woman in a past life that was highly sensitive and extremely psychic. You were once involved in a spiritual hierarchy, such as a High Priestess, a practising white witch within a coven, an occultist within a Mystery School, or a spiritualist or medium. You were taught the mysteries of life, how to use and apply magic. However, at one stage in your spiritual development you misused your arcane knowledge and psychic skills for personal self-gain and this halted future progress.

You have now reached a karmic crossroads and have another opportunity to develop your psychic nature. Mediation and studying holistic subjects will recall the inner-knowledge that you have inherited and karmic development will come through selflessly applying your skills to serve others. Using your intuitive nature for the greater good will dissipate and clear karmic residue. Raising your consciousness to a higher vibration will give a deep a profound understanding of the Divine Feminine, lunar consciousness and the mysterious cycles of life.

MERCURY IN THE EIGHTH HOUSE
MALE INCARNATION

Astrological tradition describes those with Mercury in the eighth house as being highly secretive and curious with a probing mind. Druidic Soul Star explains why such astrological conclusions were reached. Mercury's karmic placement reveals that you are secretive about your plans and personal ambitions because during a previous life someone you trusted and confided in betrayed you. Now you find it difficult to trust and hence the secrecy.

Today you have the innate ability to ferret out secrets and the hidden agendas of others as you are fearful of being deceived. Mercury's spiritual light can heal your karmic mistrust if you are willing to overtly communicate and confide in others. Karmic opportunities that encourage trust may manifest as a business partnership or a situation where trust and understanding is central to mutual success.

Mercury's karmic energies give you analytical and intellectual skills, which have a transformative quality that can inspire others to change their lives. In a past life you were a writer and a teacher and you have inherited the ability to encourage others to develop their talents. You also had mediumistic and clairvoyant skills and the ability to communicate with the Spiritual realms; you have inherited these psychic abilities.

MERCURY RETROGRADE MOTION

During one incarnation the separation or the death of a brother, sister or close friend caused an emotional trauma. The shock reside may have caused a psychic-block in the throat chakra which could manifest as nervousness or breathing problems such as asthma. Alternatively, you may find communicating with others, working in large groups and promoting yourself challenging. Your karmic lesson is to believe in yourself and let your intuition guide you towards love, trust and understanding.

VENUS IN THE EIGHTH HOUSE
FEMALE INCARNATION

Venus in this placement offers spiritual growth through your emotional relationships.

In a previous life, you experienced financial gains through marriage, partnerships or a business venture. Wishing to help others you shared your resources and now the warm rays of Venus offer beneficial karma often manifesting as an inheritance, the success of a business or romantic partnership or an artistic venture that will prove profitable.

You have inherited a sensual, loving nature and a creative or artistic gift. You have the ability to see beauty where others do not. You have a loving heart and your strong feeling nature and deep emotions require a sensitive and caring partner who will understand your depth of feeling. Romantic and social relationships are especially important to you. Venus in the eighth house often indicates that you will find your soul mate.

VENUS RETROGRADE MOTION

In a recent past life you experienced severe financial hardship, which may have been caused, for instance, by a marriage ending unfairly, or you may have lost your inheritance, possessions or property due to the actions of others who conspired against you resulting in destitution.

You karmic passage through time has heightened your appreciation of the material world in which you live and you value relationships far greater than material possessions. Your karmic lesson is to learn to trust others.

MARS IN THE EIGHTH HOUSE
MALE INCARNATION

Mars in the eighth house exerts a powerful influence because astrologically this house is ruled by Mars and corresponds to the sign of Scorpio.

Presenting challenging karma, Mars reveals that in a previous life you were a male with a headstrong and impulsive nature. Strong sexual desires and emotions coupled with a forceful attitude enabled you to get what you wanted when you wanted it!

In this incarnation, you are being encouraged to express your emotions in a gentler manner and to restrain headstrong and impulsive tendencies. You can grow spiritually by relinquishing the desire to dominate or control. Conversely, you may attract a forceful partner and therefore need to be fully aware of these karmic undercurrents.

You have also inherited positive traits; you are bold and spirited. Provided your emotions are balanced, you should experience general good health throughout this incarnation. However, unbalanced emotions will cause high blood pressure, fevers, irritating rashes or accidents.

Ruling death and rebirth, this esoteric house can describe the circumstances surrounding a previous death. In many cases, Mars in this placement indicates military activity caused a violent death through war or conflict.

MARS RETROGRADE MOTION

This placement suggests a past life where a strong sexual nature became unbalanced and lustful self-gratification prevailed. To rebalance the karma and understand the lesson, love should be encouraged to blossom and inner anger dispelled.

Retrograde Mars reveals that you once experienced an unlawful imprisonment or a sudden and violent death. A birthmark may indicate the area of the body that experienced the violent impact.

JUPITER IN THE EIGHTH HOUSE
MALE OR FEMALE INCARNATION

Jupiter brings a karmic blessing and spiritual integrity. Over several past lives you have studied and experienced many different religions including metaphysical disciplines and you travelled extensively. Thus, you are now exceptionally tolerant of cultural differences and the religious belief systems of others. Additionally, past life experiences with the Christian clergy provided you with good morals and ethics. You have gained a deep and philosophical understanding of the world in which you live. You are an old soul.

In this incarnation, you have an expansive and compassionate understanding of other peoples' feelings and well-developed psychic awareness. Your consciousness is being raised to a higher level as there is spiritual work for you to do. You may be drawn to study alternative healing techniques, metaphysical disciplines, astrology or yoga. Alternatively, you may travel to the countries where you once experienced a profound connection. By reconnecting to the past through study or travel, you will receive spiritual nourishment and wisdom.

This esoteric placement of Jupiter indicates that in a past life you were spiritually blessed, had a full life and died peacefully due to natural causes. You are twice blessed if you stay on a positive karmic path.

JUPITER RETROGRADE MOTION

In a previous life, you had an extravagant and flamboyant nature and may have inherited the desire to overspend and indulge yourself! You also used other people's resources for your own pleasure and entertainment, as you were a social butterfly. Your karmic lesson is not to over indulge yourself but to seek temperance and balance.

During one past life you were mentally talented and highly creative, yet you did nothing with the gift. The main soul teaching Jupiter brings is not to be wasteful of your resources – no matter what they are – your relationships, ideas or possessions. You have another opportunity to develop your creativity. This time do not blow it by doing nothing.

SATURN IN THE EIGHTH HOUSE
MALE INCARNATION

Many life times ago, in the distant past, you were a spiritual teacher or a high-ranking member of the priesthood. Your wisdom and timeless advice was sought by many and you became well known and respected. In this incarnation, you could easily tap into that ancient wisdom which lies within your soul, and allow it to become your guiding light.

You were also successful at creating financial prosperity for yourself and others. You were once responsible for your own, as well as other people's finances, and may have worked in the banking, insurance or property sectors. Equally as likely, you were a trader, merchant, landlord or held stewardship of the land.

In this incarnation you have inherited similar skills, such as money management and resourcefulness, as well as a sense of justice when dealing with other peoples' assets. You have integrity and an honest nature and may find yourself being accountable for other people's property as well as your own.

Often this placement indicates that during your Soul's journey a death was caused by a long-term illness. Karmic residue may persist as a fear of death or disturbing repetitive dreams.

SATURN RETROGRADE MOTION

In a previous life, you experienced serious problems relating to property, inheritance and joint business ventures. Possibly, in the same life, or during another incarnation, you married an older person and shouldered great financial responsibilities and severe hardship. Thus, in this incarnation you are especially frugal and skilful at managing your resources. Your karmic lesson is to understand the value of money as you have endured financial limitations in the past. You will growth both materially and spiritually in this incarnation if you share your resources rather than hold onto them.

URANUS IN THE EIGHTH HOUSE
MALE INCARNATION

In a previous life, you experienced sudden changes in your fortune, perhaps due to an unexpected inheritance, business venture or marriage. At one stage, the changes were beneficial and you rose to great prominence, then a dramatic financial reversal caused poverty and suffering. Remaining unresolved, past karmic residue may resurface during this incarnation as a sudden change of circumstances. Creating financial stability, and not frittering away your assets and personal resources, is the key to resolving the karma. Failure to do so will cause a perpetual karmic cycle of financial highs and lows.

On a spiritual level, you have inherited psychic ability and you know there is life after death. Uranus is often associated with group karma; you, your friends or colleagues may have shared a karmic experience together. You also have a karmic bond with a special friend.

The eighth house is the house of death and rebirth. Uranus' placement indicates that a previous life ended suddenly probably caused by an accident. Due to your inherent sensitive nature, there is often foreknowledge of the conditions and time of death…

URANUS RETROGRADE MOTION

During one particular past life, you experienced an unconventional lifestyle; you were exceptionally radical and fiercely independent. Strong resonate energies associated with your sense of independence prevail and you need to feel free and unconstrained. You suit self-employment as being tied to a routine job may stifle your sense of freedom. You may choose to live or work with a group of likeminded people to develop new ideologies.

You have inherited intense psychic sensitivity, telepathic skills and the ability to remote view. However, past misuse means such skills have lain dormant for centuries. An honest heart and right motive are the only requirements for you to become a powerful light worker.

NEPTUNE IN THE EIGHTH HOUSE
FEMALE INCARNATION

This placement occurs in the charts of those who have reached a high level of spiritual awareness. Over the duration of several lifetimes, one of which goes back millennia, you have studied the psychic arts.

You were once a medium who communicated with those who passed over to the other side. You reached great heights and your mediumship skills were well known. You had clairvoyant skills, the ability to access inner and outer dimensions and create time portals.

Invariably, with Neptune in this position you probably experienced a paranormal encounter during your childhood. For instance, you may have seen or interacted with the angelic or elemental kingdoms. Alternatively, you may have seen a ghost, or heard voices from beyond the third dimension. The event was reminding you of your inborn sensitivity and psychic ability - your karmic gift.

If you choose to do so, you can use your psychic ability to help others. Many ancient seers, magicians and witches are today's psychotherapists, counsellors and healers.

Traditionally, Neptune in the eight house suggests death in a previous life occurred during the sleep, a karmic blessing for utilizing your psychic gifts and helping others for the greater good.

NEPTUNE RETROGRADE MOTION

In a former life, you experienced martial difficulties and financial losses through deception, fraud or the illegal activity caused by yourself or others. Therefore, in this incarnation your karmic lesson is to pay attention to your finances and make sure that everything is honest and lawful.

In a distant life, you misused your psychic powers for personal gain and greed. If your sensitive nature is resurfacing, make sure you do not make the same mistake, as karmic temptation will test you. You have the opportunity to gain prominence as a psychic, writer or actor.

PLUTO IN THE EIGHTH HOUSE
MALE OR FEMALE INCARNATION

Pluto is powerfully placed in the eighth house because Pluto rules this house which corresponds to the sign of Scorpio.

Over many lives, you have developed your spiritual nature and attained higher consciousness. In previous lives, you studied and taught astrology, yoga, healing and other esoteric subjects. You were a great teacher of the Mysteries of Life.

With Pluto in this position, you understand human nature and may have interests in psychotherapy or sociology. You are an old soul and your spirit guides have been with you for centuries and are willing to help you in unseen ways. Your high spiritual protection allows you to walk where others fear to tread. But be careful and tread with due care.

In this lifetime, you have the ability to be highly intuitive or clairvoyant, have the gift to see auras and channel information and energy. Your Soul contract is to help others to transform their lives and your natural teaching skills are one of your greatest assets. You may sense that you are here for a reason. You are.

PLUTO RETROGRADE MOTION

In a past life serious problems concerning your partner's money or inheritance caused despair. The karmic memory could make you anxious or fearful when dealing with relationship problems or marital possessions. However, if you encounter this, or a similar karmic lesson, you have the ability to alchemically transform the problem by looking within for the answer.

Pluto in the eight house indicates that in a previous life you were a master of the occult arts. However, the retrograde motion reveals misuse of occult power. Unconditionally helping others to overcome their problems will release long forgotten karma and allow you to reconnect to the adept within.

CHIRON IN THE EIGHTH HOUSE

In a past life your path of healing and initiation involved some sort of a struggle with the issues of the desire for sex, money, power or immortality.

In a past life you had an extremely perceptive awareness of other people's desires, and can read people at the deepest level. The lesson in this life is not to be tempted to use this inherited skill to manipulate or control others, as in a past life you had an obsessive need for power and control.

Your spiritual lesson involves releasing childhood trauma energy, so that you can heal the child within. This will lead to a transformation that empowers you. Past understanding and your century's old great wisdom will rise to the surface to guide you. With this placement, it is especially important not to give your power away to a 'master', guru or teacher as your inner self is the True Master and Teacher.

CHIRON IN THE EIGHTH HOUSE
RETROGRADE MOTION. MALE INCARNATION

In a past life you experienced desires such as needing sex, money, and power. The karmic lesson of this position is mastery over the desire nature which will result in a deep and eternal wisdom.

In a life that you lived before this one, you had a penetrating mind and an innate understanding of primal life forces. An important karmic lesson is never to misuse your power to manipulate others again. Develop self-discipline and attain a higher consciousness. You have spirit guides by your side waiting to help you gain spiritual awareness to share with others.

On an esoteric level, you were taught many different divination systems and today you will have interests in divination systems, such as tarot or astrology.

Chapter Eight
Planets In The Twelfth House

*T*he twelfth house is an important part of the Druidic Soul Star chart as it is one of the petals of the flowering lotus. It corresponds to the zodiac sign of Pisces, which is the last sign of the zodiac symbolising the ending of a karmic cycle. Planets in this house reveal how we can end old karmic cycles or habits so that we can face a new and brighter future. Planets in this sector represent deep rooted and ancient karma often associated with fear or conflict. Invariably, planets in the twelfth house signify very distant past lives showing that you are an old soul with inherited occult and metaphysical knowledge.

SUN IN TWELFTH HOUSE
MALE INCARNATION

If you have the Sun in the twelfth house, you have the inner need to serve others, as part of your soul contract is to help others. In a past life, you spent time alone to study and explore the Mysteries of Life. Due to this reclusive behaviour, which could go on for months at a time, there will be times in your current incarnation when you desire to seek seclusion from the world.

However, because you spent time alone in a previous life, you may lack confidence in your current abilities and may feel, at times, inferior.

Yet, you are deeply aware of the undercurrents that silently influence people's lives and you have an empathy with others, especially the sick or the venerable. You have inherited clairvoyant powers and if you choose to develop this aspect of yourself, previous psychic awareness and knowledge will raise your consciousness.

MOON IN TWELFTH HOUSE
FEMALE INCARNATION

The Moon in the twelfth house indicates that in a previous life you have served others and worked behind the scenes in an institution, hospital or even a jail. This may have been in medieval times or even as late as the Victorian or Edwardian eras. You certainly once had dealings with the public's welfare or those unfortunates of life. Your soul asked to continue this work in this incarnation. You feel some sort of cross to bear due to your karmic responsibility, which others may not be aware of, and so it is important to voice your feelings and thoughts – no matter how profound they are.

There may be karma between you and your mother, or you and your child/daughter, and this bond was forged centuries ago. If your mother caused you some distress in this life, there may be the need to resolve the past conflict or karma. Later, we will explore some healing techniques.

MERCURY IN TWELFTH HOUSE
MALE OR FEMALE INCARNATION

You have inherited from a previous life a perceptive, intuitive and sharp mind with an interest in the metaphysical world. You can absorb knowledge intuitively and you understand more than you wish to divulge. You may have learnt form the great libraries of Alexandria in Egypt, as Mercury is associated with Egypt's deep wisdom. However, you were taught certain mysteries that were not known to the general population and so in this incarnation you are secretive and have the ability to understand the deeper meanings of the life.

MERCURY RETROGRADE MOTION

As you once worked behind the scenes and away from the public eye, you may in this incarnation lack confidence in yourself, as you were not used to socializing. This may have been apparent as you were growing up especially in your early teens with a tendency towards shyness.

In this previous incarnation, you once worked hard and long hours. Today, you may find yourself limited, or incapacitated, if you allow your nerves to become too overworked or overstrained.

A karmic affliction may be associated with your ears affecting your hearing, which may be weaker than average.

VENUS IN TWELFTH HOUSE
FEMALE INCARNATION

If you incarnated with Venus in the twelfth house of your Druidic Soul Star karmic chart, you like solitude and being in your own company.

There were times when you wanted to retreat from society and this characteristic still prevails.

In the past, you once practiced the psychic or occult arts. Therefore, healing and seeing beyond the third dimension will come naturally to you, as within the Soul memory you understand the unseen realms of life.

You have inherited a strong sense of compassion and a willingness to help and serve others. Certainly, you have healing ability which you may choose to develop in this lifetime.

VENUS RETROGRADE MOTION

In a past life, you wanted to understanding the meaning of life, but got very confused and sort the help of others who did not have your best interest at heart. The company you kept led you down a downward spiral, and self-indulgence through drink, drugs or sex bought about self-undoing.

In a past life you had a tendency to keep your relationships with the opposite sex a secret and today you may continue this trait. Also, in the past you were betrayed by someone you loved dearly, and this is why you seldom reveal your innermost feelings. If this is the case, you need to be more open about your feelings. Your Soul lesson is to learn to love and to trust again…

MARS IN TWELFTH HOUSE
MALE INCARNATION

Incarnating with Mars in the twelfth house suggests that you have inherited intense emotional reactions and perhaps repressed desires or paranoia which can sometimes make you feel isolated and alone.

In a past life you may have experienced a betrayal – being wrongly accused of something that you did not do. Therefore, in this life you may be subject to false accusations by hidden enemies as psychic residue may surface. If this is the case, in a quiet moment let go of the fear and forgive. This simple act will initiate an energetic change and herald a new beginning.

You have inherited a love of working in secret or behind the scenes. Today you have the energy to work long and hard hours to achieve success.

MARS RETROGRADE MOTION

In a past life you spent time in solitude and worked alone. You suffered from slander and felt hurt and totally rejected. Thus, in this life you may, from time to time, feel alone and you may need to overcome deep, hidden, inner fears or resentments. If you resonate with this, or you want to overcome fear, anxiety or unbalanced emotions, direct your energy toward gaining an understanding of the meaning of life, create a balanced mindset as well as harmonic surroundings as you are highly sensitive to your environment. You will find that this will help to dissipate and heal karmic residue. Following this path will greatly enhance your life and sense of purpose.

JUPITER IN TWELFTH HOUSE

Jupiter in the twelfth house exerts a powerful influence because astrologically this house is ruled by Jupiter and corresponds to the sign of Pisces. If you have incarnated with Jupiter in the twelfth House, you have inherited a charitable and generous nature with an innate faith in the future.

In a past life, you offered your help and assistance to those that were less well off than yourself and now it is your turn to receive good fortune. You bought healing love, light, and joy into people's lives and now you have an "angel" watching over you who will assist you through hard times.

You have inherited a love of humanity and a great desire to help others, especially those who cannot fend for themselves.

Jupiter's energy imparts success which will come in a quiet and unassuming manner in the middle of your life.

JUPITER RETROGRADE MOTION

As stated above but the Soul lesson is to learn to be realistic. It is important to think all ideas through before carrying them out and learn the art of discrimination.

SATURN IN TWELFTH HOUSE
MALE INCARNATION

Born with Saturn the Lord of Karma in the twelfth House, you have inherited a strong inner discipline and sensitivity. In a previous life you were a part of the priesthood, or a member of a metaphysical society that worked behind the scenes in secret to understand the mysteries of life. You may have inherited a love of solitude due to this former experience.

If in this incarnation you experience feelings of fear, doubt, or a lack of confidence psychic residue is surfacing, as you have a strong inner desire to make right the wrongs committed in previous lives. Thus, at times you may feel fated and need to retreat from society to understand your karmic feelings which are probably close to the mark.

Your strong inner discipline and your capability to attune to the past gives you the ability to repay your past life debts. Health problems may surface if deep fears are not worked through. Part of your Soul contract is to serve humankind in some manner.

SATURN RETROGRADE MOTION

Health problems can be experienced if subconscious karmic fears are not brought out into the open. You have a love of solitude and may prefer to work alone behind the scenes preferring not to come into contact with the general public.

Let go of any fears as they are probably imaginary, as you are highly sensitive to the thought forms of other people.

URANUS IN THE TWELFTH HOUSE
MALE INCARNATION

Uranus in the twelfth House strongly suggests that millennia ago you were highly intuitive and secretive with humanitarian ideals. Within the echelons of an ancient civilisation, you were regarded as a Seer and a Wise One. You spent many hours working alone behind the scenes to understand the mysteries of the body, mind and spirit. Today, you may have feelings of loneliness as a result of this trace memory. However, your soul retains this long lost knowledge and potentially you have great psychic or healing talent.

In this past life you worked long hours furthering your deep understanding of humankind and the sacred healing arts, but you didn't know when to stop and rest. This energy may manifest in your present incarnation as nervous difficulties. As Uranus is the Soul Awakener, you have inherited metaphysical knowledge that can be tapped into and bought into consciousness.

URANUS RETROGRADE MOTION

Millennia ago, due to working alone to further your understanding of metaphysical subjects, you now have a tremendous questioning mind that looks deeply into the meaning of life and of the imperfections you see around you.

Unresolved karmic difficulties need to be brought out and resolved. This may manifest as a feeling that *something is going to get you,* which is the karmic residue of a past situation when you were betrayed. It is as though you always have a sense of impending doom. You need to overcome this apprehension as it was born of solitude and betrayal long ago. Self-control must be developed to overcome this distant memory.

NEPTUNE IN TWELFTH HOUSE
MALE OR FEMALE INCARNATION

Neptune in the twelfth house exerts a powerful influence because astrologically this house is ruled by Neptune and corresponds to the sign of Pisces.

Neptune rules Atlantis and this placement strongly suggests that in Atlantis you were taught metaphysics and you were renowned for your psychic ability and wisdom. Your skill was known throughout Atlantis and you taught and helped others to connect to a Higher Source to become part of the Oneness of Life.

You had a deep understanding of herbs and natural lore.

Today, you are reflective, intuitive and have inherited psychic ability. You may experience intense feelings of loneliness and of being held in bondage to a specific person. This may be a trace memory of being so intimately connected to the spiritual hierarchy of Atlantis.

You still feel the need to connect to a Higher Source and to become part of the Oneness of Life, because deep within your being, you remember teaching this to others. You still have an interest in occult and mystical subjects.

NEPTUNE RETROGRADE MOTION

You may feel that you are often misunderstood as in a previous life there were complex relationship problems that led to you being alone. Therefore, you may feel that when you do enter a relationship you will be abandoned.

You have inherited psychic ability, although it may operate unconsciously and you need to learn to control this power within. You probably spent time in Atlantis and learnt the art of crystal wisdom.

PLUTO IN TWELFTH HOUSE
MALE OR FEMALE INCARNATION

Pluto in the twelfth House, indicates that millennia ago, you were possibly a government leader, a High Priest, or you once worked within a large organisation or health institute. You gave your life to that organisation in search of metaphysical truths and wonders. Thus, today when trace memories surface, you may feel that you are searching for transformation and regeneration or a long lost wisdom.

Destiny plays a role in your life and occasional upheavals, or points of crisis, manifest in order to bring you back to the correct path. Today, you still have a desire to retreat from society, unconsciously recalling your past life in the priesthood or as someone who worked long hours in contemplative solitude.

PLUTO RETROGRADE MOTION

In a distant life, you experienced poverty and felt downtrodden. You were robbed or betrayed and you may have been imprisoned, as the twelfth house rules prisons. If correct, you may dislike being in small confined spaces and fear being deceived.

Secret enemies were your undoing or there was an abuse of power related to psychic activity.

CHIRON IN THE TWELFTH HOUSE
MALE INCARNATION

In a past life you were a mystic. The twelfth house is ruled by Neptune, who connects us with the realms beyond time and space. Higher and immortal Beings can sense and feel your presence.

You were and still are deeply intuitive and aware of the non-physical realms of reality. Your mind is intensely curious and probing, and you cultivate an inner knowing born of ancient wisdom and past experiences. You have incarnated to fulfil a very high purpose. However, your path may be a difficult one, because your Soul has set the bar very high.

CHIRON IN THE TWELFTH HOUSE
RETROGRADE MOTION. MALE INCARNATION

In a past life you followed a teacher or guru believing you would receive enlightenment but you became reliant and a servant.

You are very intuitive, but you have over many past lives ignored your perceptive feelings. Your soul lesson is to develop faith in yourself and faith in your intuition.

Learn to trust your own inner guidance and inner knowing. Your intuition is sharp and at times is assisted by Higher Forces. You incarnated to fulfil a high purpose and need to overcome the challenge of the past to benefit the future.

On an esoteric level, you were taught how to communicate with plants, herbs, trees and flowers.

Chapter Nine
Planets In The Druidic Soul Star Triangle

The Druidic Soul Star triangle is the upward pointing triangle that has three sections which are the second, sixth and tenth astrological houses.

In natal astrology the second house represents money and possessions. In Druidic Soul Star astrology, its higher meaning represents spiritual values and karmic resources. Planets in this sector describe how you have experienced the material world in past lives. For instance, Saturn in this sector suggests that in a previous life you probably experienced extreme poverty or famine. Planets in this house will show you how a Soul has previously experienced the World of Matter. This house often reveals or emphasises a Spiritual Lesson or a Spiritual Value as the planets are our Teachers that impart energy and wisdom which we receive on the Soul level.

Karmic debts can manifest in our lives as repetitive behavioural patterns, meeting similar situations or coming face to face with persistent blockages. By understanding our Spiritual Lesson, we can release past karmic debts, karmic psychic residue and enduring blockages.

The sixth house in Druidic Soul Star astrology represents Spiritual Service. Often planets in this sector indicate that you have worked on a spiritual level in previous lives and have inherited healing abilities. This sector can also reveal any past life psychic residue that may be influencing your health. In natal astrology this house represents your job, personal service and health.

The third and highest section of the Druidic Soul Star triangle corresponds to the tenth house. In natal astrology, the tenth house relates to the career as well as professional and public reputation.

Druidic Soul Star astrology transforms this mundane meaning and describes your highest spiritual goals, karmic responsibilities and hidden talents or gifts. Many people with planets in this sector are Old Souls and have incarnated to help Mankind ascend to a higher level. It can also describe your Guardian Angel, Spirit Guides and those Higher Beings that want to share their light and understanding with you.

PLANETS IN THE SECOND HOUSE

SUN IN SECOND HOUSE
MALE INCARNATION

If you have incarnated with the Sun in the second house, in a previous life you were generous and ambitious, and you had a strong sense of self-worth. You worked hard and gained personal material possessions, talents and money. You understood that money brings freedom and so in this life money may come and go easily.

Today, a spiritual valve to be applied is not to be extravagant and grasping. A karmic lesson is not to be possessive of people and things. This is because at one point in a past life you did not feel loved or feel worthy of love. The Sun in the second karmic house sends a simple message - love yourself.

MOON IN SECOND HOUSE
FEMALE INCARNATION

Shining light upon a spiritual lesson, the Moon in the second house teaches that you do not need money or possessions for your emotional security. However, contradicting this, your feelings and sense of emotional well-being may be connected with your material resources.

This is because in a former life, you went though a lot of financial changes, upheavals and fluctuations which made you feel very insecure and unworthy of love. Today, when this trace memory resurfaces, you may alternate between being thrifty and careless with your money. Balance is therefore needed.

You have a strong desire to identify with your work and to be financially stable to provide for your family. This is not a 'bad' thing; however, remember to love yourself for who you are rather than for what you have. Your Karmic Lesson is to have self-worth.

MERCURY IN SECOND HOUSE
MALE INCARNATION

Mercury in the second House shows that in a past life you had an innate ability to communicate and you were a natural writer or a speaker. You had the knowledge and versatility to accumulate wealth. However, you neglected those you loved in your pursuit of material rewards. The result was loneliness despite the fact you were successful. And this soul lesson may still apply.

Today, you have the inherited ability to communicate ideas to others through writing and speaking. You may have financial skill, but your money may come and go, regardless. Until you learn to balance love and money this karmic cycle will be in perpetual motion. The spiritual valve you need to apply is to seek material balance.

MERCURY RETROGRADE MOTION

You were very mercurial with money and your resources in the past. Certainly, money came and went. You had no regard for money or property and felt free to come and go as you pleased. If there is a trace memory of this then freedom is important to you. Learning to be careful and respectful of money, which is just energy, may be a lesson that still persists across the mists of time.

VENUS IN SECOND HOUSE
FEMALE INCARNATION

Venus in the second house exerts a powerful influence because astrologically this house is ruled by Venus and corresponds to the sign of Taurus.

If you have incarnated with Venus in the second house you have learnt a valuable soul lesson that love is greater than material possessions.

During a past life, you gave generously to those around you and you shared your possessions. This is why in this life you attract money and personal possessions, especially when needed.

VENUS RETROGRADE MOTION

You may spend money as fast as you can earn it, and you may be attracted to buying beautiful, artistic, or musical things. You like a certain degree of luxury because in a former life you were surrounded by beautiful objects. In a past life relationship or marriage, good karma was forged, as you gave money to the person you loved which helped them considerably. What goes around comes around, and so in this life, money may come to you through a partner or relationship. A spiritual lesson is to valve people rather than objects and to realise that you have a beautiful spiritual side that seeks expression.

MARS IN SECOND HOUSE
MALE INCARNATION

In a past life you had trouble controlling your spending habits and as a result you are likely to be an impulsive shopper today!

Saving is certainly not your best strength, but you should try to improve your savings ability as it symbolises stability. During a past life you would have benefited from being able to live on your savings but you had none and it left you feel depressed. As a result of feeling destitute, your emotional self-worth may be wrapped up in your ability to make money. You may have a deep karmic fear that you will be abandoned or left destitute.

You were born with a talent or a gift and have the energy and the inner strength to achieve great success.

A spiritual lesson may manifest from time to time; money may come and go in order to de-emphasize its importance and you should concentrate on developing your talents instead.

MARS RETROGRADE MOTION

Mars gives you the spiritual lesson of values. What do you value? If emphasis is on material issues these will come and go, there will be moments of feeling especially high, and then you will feel low. When you learn to balance your material resources with good spiritual values your life will take you on a new path. You will have a far more balanced life and find love that stays and does not disappear.

JUPITER IN SECOND HOUSE
MALE INCARNATION

Money seems to come to you and you have probably never missed a meal in your life. This is because in a former life, you were especially generous and giving to your family, friends and you also helped people who were less fortunate than you were. You realized a spiritual lesson; that love is behind giving and by helping others you are helping yourself, as there is no separation; we are all universally connected.

Today, you have the ability to be financially successful. You have the confidence and optimism in your talents, and your visionary ideas, and investments usually prosper due to your intuitive appraisal of situations. Others see you as "lucky" but this is your karmic reward. You inspire trust in others, as you want them to benefit financially to make their families and loved one more comfortable.

JUPITER RETROGRADE MOTION

It seems that you constantly need assistance from others in order to develop your visionary and idealistic ideas. This may be due to the fact that you were extravagant or unreliable in a past life. You had wealth but squandered it and so in this life it is about applying a set of spiritual values and once applied your material and spiritual life will blossom.

SATURN IN SECOND HOUSE
MALE OR FEMALE INCARNATION

If you have Saturn in this House, there is always a trace memory of poverty that was experienced in a past life. You may have been left destitute and so there may be a fear of loosing everything or losing the one you love, your job or your home.

In this life, you tend to be thrifty, practical and responsible, especially with money and possessions, as you unconsciously fear loosing them again. Sometimes you are so busy squirreling away money that you forget to enjoy it.

Saturn, Lord of Karma, is a Great Teacher who brings a spiritual lesson which will probably surface as a tendency to become depressed over material matters. Feelings of being unloved, unwanted, and unappreciated occur with this planetary position. Thus, the spiritual lesson is to value yourself and do not judge yourself on your material possessions. Love yourself.

SATURN RETROGRADE MOTION

This karmic placement does not deny money, but you must work hard for it. Your possessions are apt to bring worries rather than happiness because you may need to learn to share them with others. There may have been too much emphasis on materialism in past lives.

You may need to re-evaluate your values. Attitudes of possessiveness toward others must be changed. Feelings of being unloved, unwanted, and unappreciated occur with this position. You must value yourself before others can value you. Love yourself.

URANUS IN SECOND HOUSE
MALE OR FEMALE INCARNATION

In a past life you earned money in original and inventive ways and your money and possessions came and went suddenly in peculiar or unexpected ways.

There may be unusual and disruptive changes in your financial position. The spiritual lesson that you have successfully learnt is to value money for the freedom it brings to pursue your talents, which were and still are rare and unique.

URANUS RETROGRADE MOTION

You have the ability to get yourself out of financial difficulties but you seem to repeat the same mistake and so the problem resurfaces time and time again. Uranus energy is teaching you to look long term, at the larger picture, and to attune to an inherited talent. Once utilized, your karmic talent may even help humanitarian issues. You have a lot to give.

NEPTUNE IN SECOND HOUSE
MALE OR FEMALE INCARNATION

In a previous life, you tapped into your strong imagination and psychic sensitivity. You were once trained to develop your keen intuition which was accompanied by vivid dreams that you could interpret. All these traits you have inherited as well as the deep appreciation of all that is living.

Millennia ago, you attuned to the value of life, the meaning of Universal Oneness and this has stayed with you across the eons of time.

In this life, on an inner level, you still recall those spiritual teachings imparted all that time ago and so you seldom worry about money, even if your finances are complicated and sometimes a little confusing!

NEPTUNE RETROGRADE MOTION

Due to past life residue you may be undisciplined with money and your material possessions. In a past life, you were either extremely generous or extremely dishonest. If dishonesty occurred, you will experience losses through theft, fraud and deception. Do everything above board and money matters will run smoothly. Avoid risky speculations and investments as karmic energy prevails which may hinder the process. Be completely honest with respect to money matters and any residue will dissipate.

If you were generous in a past life, you will find yourself being in the right place at the right time. Spiritual beings watch over you and are always there to assist you. In this life, you should be able to make your living from developing your creative or psychic nature.

PLUTO IN SECOND HOUSE
MALE OR FEMALE INCARNATION

If you have Pluto in the second House, in a past life you had leadership qualities as well as keen judgment, patience, and the will and power to make manifest your dreams and visions. You have inherited these characteristics as well as an unusual talent.

A spiritual lesson is to balance your desire for money and possessions, otherwise, you may see money coming and going in order to de-emphasize its importance. You may also need to watch for the tendency to view loved ones as your possessions. Detachment and learning to share your possessions with others will help resolve this karmic issue.

PLUTO RETROGRADE MOTION

As described above, but with the added emphasises that you need to practice integrity in money matters. In a past life, you controlled other people's resources and now in this lifetime, others may seek to control your resources and possessions-even you.

Alternatively, you may be quite demanding and controlling with your own resources. If this is the case, learn to seek harmony, balance and share your possessions and you will realize the joy and happiness that sharing brings.

CHIRON IN THE SECOND
MALE INCARNATION

You have inherited a very beautiful, compassionate and giving nature. In a past life, you had high values and you were a talented healer. However, today you have a deep need to define and express your values, which could manifest as a tendency to express strong opinions and judgments. Your spiritual lesson is to listen to the opinions of others and respect the values of all people and cultures.

CHIRON IN THE SECOND HOUSE
RETROGRADE MOTION. MALE INCARNATION.

In a past life you felt undervalued and you constantly tried hard to please others. You were diligent and hard working. Yet, other people always seemed to complain about your work leaving you feeling, at times, worthless.

In this life you need to realise that you are an amazing, caring and loving person. You have a warm and open heart. If other people, at times, project the karmic past upon you, realise that you have great worth and through your giving nature like the eagle you will rise and fly high.

On an esoteric level, you have been given the gift of being able to hear or see into other time dimensions. You will be attracted to sacred sites that have portals. Here the Seers of old communed beyond time and space.

Chapter Ten
Planets In The Sixth House And Karmic Health

In natal astrology the sixth house represents your job, personal service and health. In Druidic Soul Star astrology, this house represents Spiritual Service and reveals inherited healing abilities. This sector also reveals any past life karmic residue that may be influencing your health in this incarnation.

SUN IN SIXTH HOUSE
MALE INCARNATION

If you have incarnated with the Sun in the sixth house you have served others before and this placement brings a karmic solar blessing. In a past life, you were faithful, diligent and loyal to those you loved. You once held a position of authority and exercised leadership over others but with servitude and fairness, and today you have inherited these karmic traits.

You took great pride in your work which was probably in a warm or hot climate. Today, you are very happy when you are busy and you hate being bored. Because of your hard working legacy of the past, it is important that you do not overwork yourself today.

However, the Sun in this position suggests that you should take care of your physical body. You also need to note that worry and anxiety, especially over the desire to do things perfectly, can be detrimental to your health.

In a past life, you may have been a healer that took exceptional care in your work. You have inherited the gift of healing; but because you were so conscientious in the past, you need to learn how to relax, and let go off stress and tension. It's OK not to be perfect!

POSSIBLE KARMIC HEALTH ALIMENTS

The Sun rules the heart, general vitality and the back, especially the spine. The Sun rules the right eye in a man and the left eye in a woman. The Sun has rulership over Leo, the sign that governs the 5th house in the natural zodiac. Any health issues associated to these areas are probably rooted in this past life.

MOON IN SIXTH HOUSE
FEMALE INCARNATION

In a previous life you were considerate of other people, you encouraged others to make the most of themselves and now in return you have a karmic lunar blessing. You once worked as part of a Soul Group in healing or divination, or a combination of both, and enjoyed cooperating with others. Today, service to others is a good outlet for your personality.

The trace memories of working and living in cooperation with a Soul Group can make you unconsciously wish and long for the past. This may manifest as moodiness and sensitivity. Your emotions can influence your health and well-being and fluctuations in health are possible, mostly due to worry and feelings of insecurity.

In this incarnation, you may experience many job changes as you are striving to find out what you want to do. In the past, you worked with the public, with women or with young children. Public service or working with women in this incarnation would be ideally suited to your spiritual heritage as your past achievements could once again shine.

POSSIBLE KARMIC HEALTH ALIMENTS

The Moon rules the stomach as well as our gut reactions. It also rules the breasts, the left eye in a man and the right eye in a woman. In transcendental astrology the Moon is associated with the physical world and rules fluids and the etheric part of the aura.

Due to your conscientious working ethos born centuries ago, and the inner desire to bring out the best in others, you can harbour emotional tension. This may surface in this incarnation as digestive troubles which indicate the need to relax and to stop worrying.

Try not eat when you feel overworked, overtired, or when you are upset and feeling emotional. Watch your diet. You can be absorbed within your work and can be a workaholic.

MERCURY IN SIXTH HOUSE
MALE OR FEMALE INCARNATION

Mercury in the sixth house exerts a powerful influence because astrologically this house is ruled by Mercury and corresponds to the sign of Virgo.

In a past life, you had an incredible analytical ability and you may have worked in fields such as healing, medicine or the sciences; you may still be interested in these subjects. In a previous incarnation, you were prone to working exceptional hard and continually multi-tasked, working long hours and you liked order and tidiness.

In this incarnation, if you are around chaotic energies or untidiness you will feel unbalanced as this goes against your spiritual nature.

MERCURY RETROGRADE MOTION

Focusing on one job, or holding down a job for a prolonged period, may be difficult for you as you easily get restless, bored and want to experience something new. This is because in a previous life, you travelled and experienced different cultures and learnt new ways of doing things and life was full of change and excitement. Thus in this life, you may be restless with a desire for frequent job changes. Variety in your work or workplace will overcome your restless tendencies.

Previously, you have worked in areas of health and diet which probably still interest you.

POSSIBLE KARMIC HEALTH ALIMENTS

Mercury rules the lungs, respiratory system, speech impediments and other problems with the mouth and tongue. It also rules the arms, hands, shoulders, the nervous system and illnesses related to them.

Any health issues associated to these areas are probably rooted in this past life.

You will find that if you become too concerned with details, your nerves will become frayed, thus causing health problems.

VENUS IN SIXTH HOUSE
FEMALE INCARNATION

In a previous life you were very diplomatic and you were always kind, caring, fair and just to all, and because of this you now have a karmic blessing. As you helped others, and changed people's lives, your karmic blessing bestows reasonably good health, unless you abuse your body through self-indulgence such as rich and sweet foods.

You stood up for what you believed in such as releasing people from slavery or bondage.

You have inherited a great gift, you can be a great mediator when differences of opinion occur and you can bring peace and understanding to most situations. The energy of Venus, the Divine Feminine, is with you and can be called upon to assist you in times of concern.

VENUS RETROGRADE MOTION

In order to spiritually evolve, your Soul accepted a demanding set of circumstances. You chose to be in a working environment that was harsh and unbearable. You wanted to express your creative energies yet these steps were thwarted and your health suffered as a result.

The hard laborious work that you endured may still have a trace memory and in this incarnation you may wish to have a less strenuous job or to continue to work long and hard hours.

POSSIBLE KARMIC HEALTH ALIMENTS

Venus rules the kidneys, blood sugar and diabetes (Venus rules sugar) as well as illness related to sexual activity.

Due to the laborious workload that you endured in a past life, when you feel overworked or stressed your health will decline. Should this occur, you need to rest and let go of any stress and tension. Your body will react well to therapeutic massage, as you tend to hold tension in the neck and shoulder areas.

Also, you may suffer from emotional anxiety by feeling 'unworthy' and you could go through phases of feeling blocked. Creative expression will allow those energies to flow and you will find great happiness.

MARS IN SIXTH HOUSE
MALE INCARNATION

Mars in the sixth house denotes that in a past life you were highly energetic on all levels, emotionally, mentally and sexually. You may have worked within a large organisation, or in the military. Or, you may have worked alongside a large work force, like the building of the pyramids, mounds or megalithic monuments or the colossal building programmes like those of ancient Rome, Greece and India.

In this past life you were courageous, dynamic and strong; a trait that is imbedded deep within the Soul. However, you were easily irritated and impatient with anyone who was not as quick thinking as you were. Thus, in this life, you have inherited strength but also impatience and you cannot tolerate slowness on any level.

MARS RETROGRADE MOTION

In a past life, you were a hard worker but you were intolerable of those who were not. This resulted in disputes and conflicts with others, including family members. Due to the arguments and conflicts, a sense of isolation and feeling misunderstood developed. Also, you suffered from ill health or you sustained an injury through an accident, which may be seen as a birthmark.

You may have worked alongside a large work force, like the building of the pyramids, mounds or megalithic monuments or the colossal building programmes like those of ancient Rome, Greece and India.

Today, your Soul Lesson is to exercise patience and caution. Also, you need to kerb the tendency to overwork which could lead to exhaustion triggering ill health, and past injury traumas, such as back or neck ache.

POSSIBLE KARMIC HEALTH ALIMENTS

Mars rules the head, blood and muscles. Aliments such as migraines, injuries to the head, burns, inflammation, fevers and rashes have their roots in past life trauma.

Generally, you have inherited good health and strong recuperative powers for your past hard work and labour. However, Mars in this house position brings the tendency to run fevers, perhaps higher than normal, when ill.

There is a danger of burns, scalds, and accidents sustained in the course of work or employment because of wanting to get something done quickly, acting on impulse, haste, and impatience, which are your inherited traits.

JUPITER IN SIXTH HOUSE
MALE INCARNATION

Jupiter in the sixth house is a karmic blessing that tends to bestow good health. In fact, in a previous life your health problems were caused by extravagance, over-indulgence and far too much of a good thing! And this trace memory is carried over today!

Your past life blessing was earned because you were always helpful to others and you were a dependable person with a strong sense of loyalty. You inspired cooperation and good will amongst others. You were honest and fair and your have inherited these traits.

In the distant past, you also practiced healing the mind and body, and no doubt, you still have an interest in spiritual or holistic practices. Your healing work was linked to a spiritual establishment, ancient civilsation or religion.

JUPITER RETROGRADE MOTION

In a previous life you overindulged and had a life of plenty and opulence. You were a social person always wanting to experience the finer things in life. Thus, in this incarnation you may still have these traits. The karmic lesson is to learn to control excess and live in balance with money, food and drink.

In a previous life, you may have experienced an addictive or dependency issue, so in this life be aware of this age-old memory which may lie dormant.

POSSIBLE KARMIC HEALTH ALIMENTS

Jupiter rules the hips, pelvis, liver and the sciatic nerve. It also governs illness where too much of a good thing are contributing factors.

Inherited disorders due to over eating or drinking may manifest as poor circulation or liver problems in this life. Your Karmic Lesson is to not have excess in your life but to attain balance and harmony. A good healthy diet and physical fitness would help to counteract and ease complaints.

SATURN IN SIXTH HOUSE
MALE INCARNATION

Saturn in the sixth house indicates that in a past life you once studied and practiced medicine, dietary work, or worked with food, not just physically, but metaphysically.

In a life that you lived before this one you took life very seriously. You aimed for high standards, probably became well known for your ability to heal and to ease other people's health complaints. You may have worked with herbs and have an innate understanding of natural healing. Because you took your holistic and spiritual work seriously, you overworked and at some point suffered from exhaustion.

Today, you may have inherited holistic healing interests as well as a keen and highly fanatical mind and the ability to work long and hard.

SATURN RETROGRADE MOTION

In a past life you suffered from some health issues possibly in the stomach area. Therefore, you may need to watch your diet in this lifetime as your physical body may not assimilate everything it needs from the food that you eat.

However, in the past you were a practical, conscientious, hard worker who worked with small details and you were very methodical. In this lifetime, you have inherited these traits and you should be careful not to overwork yourself to the point of exhaustion; avoid repeating this karmic pattern.

Your Karmic Lesson is to balance your work and family life. The tendency to worry and to harbour anxieties will affect your health encouraging past life residue to rise and manifest as depression and perhaps hypochondria.

POSSIBLE KARMIC HEALTH ALIMENTS

Saturn rules the bones, teeth and skin. Saturn stays in each sign approximately two and a half years and takes an average of 29 years to complete a full circuit of the zodiac.

Karmic Saturn energy may suggest stomach issues or bone aliments. Overworking in a past life may cause back and neck ache as well as joint pain in this life. A good diet and regular meals is essential as Saturn energy is prone to over working.

URANUS IN SIXTH HOUSE
MALE INCARNATION

Uranus in the sixth house suggests that in a previous life you had unique creative talents and original ideas. You were highly inventive and also intuitive with clairvoyant ability.

In a previous life you dressed in a bohemian manner and stood out from the crowd. Today, your appearance and manner of dress may still be unusual. You have inherited the ability to think originally and may like the work that requires irregular hours, is different, and has a lot of variety. You are at your best when you can be independent and be your own boss. Routine hours and a repetitive job would cause you to bore instantly as your Soul recalls the inventive ways of previous self-expression.

URANUS RETROGRADE MOTION

In a past life you were very clever and your inventive ideas were praised. You worked alone and independent of others. You may have been a part of a large workforce working on a scientific project, for example, crystal power of Atlantis, the powering of ancient sites or the alchemy-science period of medieval times. In this life, you may be impatient with others and can appear to be abrupt and detached and your Karmic Lesson is to exercise patience.

POSSIBLE KARMIC HEALTH ALIMENTS

Uranus rules the circulatory and involuntary nervous system. Strange and sudden episodes can occur regarding your health, which are rooted in a past life when you suffered from nervousness, anxiety, stress, and tension. By learning to mentally and physically relax, your health will improve dramatically.

NEPTUNE IN SIXTH HOUSE
MALE OR FEMALE INCARNATION

Neptune in the sixth house denotes that in a past life you were a spiritual worker, healer or someone that helped others regarding their health and well-being. At one point in your holistic career, you worked with animals. Today you may still have an affinity with particular animals and can perceive their thoughts and feelings.

In this lifetime, if you are not helping people, or animals, it may be difficult for you to maintain an ordinary job or to work logically and systematically. In the past, you were a spiritual person with deep knowledge which can be tapped into once more.

NEPTUNE RETROGRADE MOTION

In a past life you chose not to develop your psychic talent or healing ability. Instead, there was an episode when you overindulged in alcohol or drugs. You felt the need to escape the realties of your life and your Karmic Lesson is to face reality with a clear and balanced mind set.

You may have an innate interest in psychology as you feel the need to understand the motives of others. In this lifetime, you could expand upon your psychic nature and you must realise that you are highly sensitive.

POSSIBLE KARMIC HEALTH ALIMENTS

As a challenging karmic force, Neptune governs dreams, trances, hypnosis, drugs, alcohol, illusion and escapism. Neptune energy can cause addictions to alcohol, food or drugs, as well producing physical aliments that have a psychology origin.

You have inherited extreme sensitivity to your surroundings which must be pleasant and peaceful. If not, then you may experience unusual health difficulties, some of which may be real and some may be imaginary. Remain mindful that you are a psychic sponge that absorbs the content of atmosphere around you. Herbal healing or holistic techniques may work better for you than traditional medical drug therapy.

PLUTO IN SIXTH HOUSE
MALE OR FEMALE INCARNATION

You are an old soul. Pluto links to distant past lives and lost civilisations. Pluto is powerfully placed here indicating that in a previous life you were able to transform the lives of others through your incredible healing skill and knowledge of plants and alchemy. Thus, you have good karma and psychic-healing ability. Pluto energy taken to its highest level portends that you were, and can be again, a transformer.

You may have been a shamanic priest or just as likely a member of a Mystery School. You may have studied sound and colour vibrations and their healing attributes and understood how human thought and emotion can influence the physical body.

In this incarnation, you probably have an interest in healing or psychology as trace memories rise to your consciousness recalling a life when you miraculously transformed the lives of others.

PLUTO RETROGRADE MOTION

In your last incarnation you chose not to develop your healing gift which left a kind of 'hole' in your life. Due to this inner void you were constantly looking for *something* to make you feel fulfilled. That something was never found.

In this life you still have the healing talent and the ability to transform people's lives which will make you feel fulfilled as you are helping others.

POSSIBLE KARMIC HEALTH ALIMENTS

Pluto rules the reproductive organs, as this is where the process of life begins. Pluto also rules puberty and sexual maturity. In a past life you suffered from an illness that may have left a karmic imprint which may resurface in times of stress as an infectious or problems in the colon area.

CHIRON IN THE SIXTH HOUSE
MALE INCARNATION

You were an exceptional healer in a past life. You had a remarkable sensitivity to the energy movements in the body, and an acute intuitive awareness of how the mind and emotions affect the body. Seeing beyond this, you understood how a person's mental thought vibrations influence the solar system and beyond.

Due to your inherited knowledge of health matters, you can have hypochondriacal tendencies, because you are remembering disconnected pieces of information rather than seeing the whole picture.

CHIRON IN THE SIXTH HOUSE
RETROGRADE MOTION. MALE INCARNATION

In a past life you loved your children but the tragic onset of disease took them from you. You tried desperately to heal them as you knew the art of herbal lore yet nothing would work. It was probably the plague. You blamed yourself for their untimely death but there was nothing that you could have done. You then studied medicine and became a caring and compassionate medicine man.

In this life, trace memories may surface and you could become over fretful about your own health and your families health. You are a natural healer.

On an esoteric level, you have been given the gift of being able to assist trees; plants and Mother Nature to self heal.

POSSIBLE KARMIC HEALTH ALIMENTS

You may experience mood swings that affect your health and you are highly sensitive to lunar phases. Your chakra system is highly sensitive especially the solar plexus, heart, throat and physical complaints may surface in their corresponding physical areas. Regular clearing of the auric field and chakras will maintain balance and harmony.

Chapter Eleven
Planets In The Tenth House

The tenth house is an important sector in the Druidic Soul Star triangle as it forms one of the karmic petals of the flowering lotus.

In natal astrology, this house relates to the career, professional status and public reputation. It can also represent the parents, usually the father. Druidic Soul Star astrology transforms this mundane meaning and describes your highest spiritual goals, karmic responsibilities and hidden talents or gifts. Many people with planets in this sector are Old Souls and have incarnated to help Mankind ascend to a higher level. All of us, regardless of our astrological planetary placements have spiritual guides and we can call upon them at any time. However, the tenth house describes an intimate connection to heavenly forces, Guardian Angels, Spirit Guides and those Higher Beings that share their knowledge and bring guidance. This sacred house casts a spiritual light that can illuminate your path.

Planets in the tenth house of the Druidic Soul Star triangle indicate that your sixth sense has been encouraged to develop over several past lives. Furthermore, your unfolding seventh and eighth dimensional senses are becoming activated by the Galactic Centre. This sector reveals your karmic rewards and the benefits drawn from past life experiences. At the time of your birth, high in the heavens above your birthplace shone the planets in the tenth house. Illuminating the land below, activating your crown chakra and spiritual body, tenth house planets are radiant and can bestow profound knowledge from cosmic sources. Their planetary rays hold great potential for you to develop spiritually and grow in consciousness. Deep within your being, the universal tides of time stir reminding you of former lives and karmic talents.

Planets in the tenth house may indicate that you have lived a life as a celestial star being, or that you may have worked with the devic, angelic, elemental or fey beings. Should you choose to do so, you can attune to the highest realms of galactic energy and bring the light back to transform your life and the life of others. You are a light-caster...

SUN IN TENTH HOUSE
MALE INCARNATION

In a past life you were in a position of power and influence. Exercising rulership or authority, you were always an honest person who treated people with dignity and affection. The Sun in this position symbolises that your Soul has shone brightly in a previous life and you can now receive positive karma.

Spiritually speaking, at the time of your birth, your crown and heart chakras were illuminated and are open to earth and cosmic forces. A divine link was created to a heavenly source, such as your Guardian angel, the solar archangel Michael, a spirit guide or a star being. If you choose to work with such spiritual forces, your consciousness will expand and you will receive spiritual teachings.

A karmic link has been forged with a particular male - the father, son, grandson, uncle or partner/husband etc. You are from the same Soul Group and may share the same celestial heritage. In this incarnation, you have the ability to inspire others through your example and to be a spiritual teacher.

SOUL GUIDANCE AND GUIDES

You have a special spiritual link to the Sun, the archangel Michael and male deities and planets. You have a male spirit guide. Your soul is encouraged is to attune to higher forces and be a channel for celestial energies.

MOON IN TENTH HOUSE
FEMALE INCARNATION

In a previous life you were a Seer or a Priestess with exceptional intuition and perception. You were initiated into the Mysteries and you had natural empathy with people and nature. A karmic link ties you to women in your family, the mother, or daughter, sister, grandmother etc., all of whom were born with the gift of prophecy, although they may not have used it. You are all apart of the same Soul Group.

In this incarnation, unsure of what you should be doing with your life, you may experience many changes in your career. After your 29th birthday, you will begin to understand your Soul Purpose; apart of which is to expand your psychic, spiritual or healing gifts to help others, and to find a career path that suits your sensitivity.

In this incarnation, you have an innate ability to nurture other people's ideas and bring the best out in them. Yet sometimes you will feel inadequate and your moods will go through phases. You have the gift of the Seer and so any healing or divination system will come naturally to you, as old soul memories will recall the past and influence your future.

SOUL GUIDANCE AND GUIDES

Soul guidance encourages you to control your emotions. You have a spiritual link to Gaia, female deities, the Fey, Undines, Gnomes and feminine planets. One of your spiritual guides is a psychic female priestess.

MERCURY IN TENTH HOUSE
MALE OR FEMALE INCARNATION

Mercury at the time of your birth activated your throat chakra giving you good communication skills and the ability to teach.

In a past life, you were a metaphysical teacher and writer. You were able to energetically link into other dimensions and communicate across time. You were able to access information from the Akashic Records, to read the past and to see into the unfolding future.

These gifts may surface in this incarnation and you may be drawn to the teaching profession or you could make an excellent writer. Certainly, you have the ability to communicate your ideas and you have inherited clairaudient ability.

Previously, in a past life you travelled far and wide to understand different cultures and the energies of various lands. This may manifest in two ways: firstly, as a desire to travel in this incarnation or, secondly, as the need to settle down as your 'travelling' days are done and now you love home life and the land upon which you live.

MERCURY RETROGRADE MOTION

Mercury is associated with Egypt and North Africa, which is where a trauma caused a block to the throat chakra. After which you began to feel emotionally and mentally inadequate and unable to voice your options. You also suffered from exhaustion, felt cut off from people and unable to communicate your feelings. Dishonesty from either yourself or another caused much anxiety.

In this incarnation you may suffer from bouts of inadequacy and feel others do not understand you. Once overcome, and we will explore some healing techniques later, you will be able to express yourself and others will see a new side to you that shines Mercurial bright.

SOUL GUIDANCE AND GUIDES

Instead of alternating between being silent, or expressing yourself in an outburst of emotion, Soul guidance encourages you to communicate your thoughts and feelings in a balanced way. You have a special link to Mercury, Thoth, Hermes, Lugh and Loki. Also, to Orion, the stars of Castor and Pollox in Gemini, and the bright star Spica in Virgo.

One of your spiritual guides was once your brother or sister in a former life and, there was, and still is, a loving connection. The Air elementals or Slyphs of the Celtic Middle Kingdom resonate with your energies.

VENUS IN TENTH HOUSE
FEMALE INCARNATION

Personal and romantic relationships are especially important to you, because at the time of your birth, Venus activated your heart chakra.

In a past life you were very kind, affectionate, generous and gave your time and energy to assist others. A spiritual acknowledgement for this has now been granted giving you a magnetic personality that attracts good fortune.

In a past life, you were artistic, you have inherited this skill, and you are highly creative. You will find that people are willingly to help you as they sense whom you were and what you did in a life that was lived before this one.

There is an inner desire to find your Soul Mate and there is a strong possibility that you will meet again and share a loving relationship.

In this life, you will probably have a kind and friendly approach to the world with a general attitude of optimism. Your voice is probably soothing and kind. This position usually grants comfortable financial circumstances as a karmic reward for assisting others in the past.

VENUS RETROGRADE MOTION

In a past life you met your soul mate. However, there was a sudden separation that left you feeling abandoned or betrayed. Psychic residue may linger and manifest as a fear of trusting others, especially people close to you.

Your Karmic Lesson is to learn to trust. This may be difficult as in a past life you may have lost your social status, personal belongings and felt unworthy of a relationship.

Today, you may experience bouts of feeling lonely and misunderstood as the tides of time reflect back to a time that was. Letting go with forgiveness can grant a new beginning and by releasing old patterns, we can transform our lives anew.

SOUL GUIDANCE AND GUIDES

Soul guidance asks you to trust again. If you already have a trusting nature, you have released the 'karmic-block'. If not, you need to take the first step towards trusting which requires an open heart and faith. You have a spiritual link to female deities and the female planets of the Solar System, such as the Moon, Gaia, Ceres and feminine star systems. One of your spiritual guides is female.

MARS IN TENTH HOUSE
MALE INCARNATION

Mars at the time of your birth activated your emotional body and, or, the base chakra.

In a past life you had an ambitious and enthusiastic nature with lots of energy. You were in a position of power and authority as you had strong leadership skills. You have inherited these skills, retain leadership qualities and you can take the initiative.

You are a passionate person with high energy levels and you feel that you incarnated for a reason. Today, success will come to you through your own enterprise and self-belief as it did so before. You probably do best in an occupation with variety. Your self-reliance is strong, you are practical and results oriented. There may be some karmic energy with one of your parents or with superiors at work.

MARS RETROGRADE MOTION

In a past life, power and authority were abused, or sudden reversals in fortune were experienced. In this life, there may be a temptation to use unfair means to gain power or position; and this is a karmic test.

SOUL GUIDANCE AND GUIDES

Your Soul guidance is to avoid the desire for material wealth and power. Spiritual growth is paramount for this incarnation in order to experience well-being and good fortune.

You have a spiritual link to Mars and to the star Antares in Scorpio and Aldebaran in Taurus. One of your spiritual guides is male. The Fire elementals or Salamanders of the Celtic Middle Kingdom resonate with your energies.

JUPITER IN TENTH HOUSE
MALE INCARNATION

Jupiter at the time of your birth activated your spiritual body and throughout your many past lives, you have studied philosophy, religion and metaphysics.

Jupiter in the tenth house brings opportunity and expansion as well as success and honour in your professional life or to your family life.

This is because in a past life you were always helpful, friendly and had a very generous nature. You had a strong sense of responsibility toward your family, career and also towards other people. Thus, the lesson of karmic responsibility was learnt.

Your karmic reward is that you have been given a magnetic personality and people sense this and will not let you down. Many opportunities will arise which are of benefit to you and to society as a whole. You have the ability to get other people to believe in your expansion-oriented, long-range plans and dreams. Karma is on your side to help you to dream your dreams awake.

In a past life you held a position of high standing, or you were in a religious organisation, and you have inherited moral principles.

JUPITER RETROGRADE MOTION

In a past life there was a sudden change of fortune which led to a disgrace or fall from power. Karmic memory may persist as feelings of inferiority, hopelessness or a sense that things 'could go wrong' for you. Letting go of those thought-forms will help you gain a true perspective. Write down all your fears on a piece of paper, for example of failure, inadequacy etc., and then find a place outside and in a safe manner burn the paper and bury the ashes to symbolise burying the past.

SOUL GUIDANCE AND GUIDES

Your karmic gift is that in the latter years of your life you will have comfort and security. You have a spiritual link to Jupiter and Zeus. One of your spirit guides has a philosophical and knowledgeable nature who may have been a monk, priest, Druid or a high ranking religious person.

SATURN IN TENTH HOUSE
MALE INCARNATION

Saturn in the tenth house is powerfully placed because this house corresponds to the sign of Capricorn, which Saturn rules. Saturn is the lord of time and is the planet which holds the most elevated position in the natural zodiac. At the time of your birth, Saturn activated the spiritual bodies of your aura. Saturn exerts a powerful influence representing an important past life that holds valuable meaning.

In a past life, you were self-reliant and independent with good organization skills. You were successful and worked hard for all your achievements, and they were many. Your Soul Contract in this incarnation is to accept your responsibilities; otherwise, life will be a series of setbacks and failures.

A karmic bridge may be needed to heal a situation between you and one of your parents, as there were conflicts and difficulties in a past life. Parental issues such as discipline, strictness or the need to control your life were seeded in the distant past and need to be resolved to release the karmic binding energy. With positive intent, let the past go, as you can break the bond and the karma, with love and forgiveness.

In one past life you were initiated into the Mysteries and you were an adept. The rings of Saturn are an energetic connecting force between the inner and outer realms of the solar system. Likewise, Saturn energy connects the higher self to the personality. Within your Soul you have age-old wisdom and can access the Akashic Records as Saturn is the Lord of Time and the Key to unlocking time past to pave the way to a brighter and more fulfilling future.

With Saturn in such a prominent position, Universal energy is saying that you can rise to great heights in your chosen field or subject. You have the potential to climb the mountain of success.

SATURN RETROGRADE MOTION

In a past life you held a position of authority and power but you placed obstacles in the way of others to hold onto your authority. In this incarnation, if you are blocked, or have obstacles placed in your path, you now understand why. By acknowledging the past and forgiving past actions and wrong doings will help to clear the blockages. You have the potential to be like the mythical Phoenix and to rise from the karmic ashes to great heights and all that is required is to take the first step towards a new destiny. Take your first step now and create a new future with faith, dignity and an inner knowing the Universe is supporting you.

SOUL GUIDANCE AND GUIDES

Your karmic lesson is not to chase power or use others to get what you want; otherwise, this will ensure your downfall. You need to control your ambitions; a soul lesson is to communicate your thoughts and feelings in a softer but powerful way. You have a spiritual link to Saturn, the stars of Capricorn, the constellation of Aquilla the Eagle and the bright star Capella.

Another possible karmic lesson is to look at any issues you have with your parents and to resolve the time old pattern.

One of your spiritual guides is a wise and mature person with deep knowledge. The Earth Spirits or Gnomes resonate with your energies.

URANUS IN TENTH HOUSE
MALE OR FEMALE INCARNATION

At the time of your birth Uranus activated your Third Eye chakra and intuitive powers.

If you have Uranus in the tenth House, it reveals that in a previous life you were not a conformer and you had an unusual career. You were highly independent and maverick. You experienced sudden changes in your fortune and you hated mundane jobs and people that conformed to the 'norm'. At one time you lived in Bohemia, which means Home of the Celts.

In this life, you have inherited these traits and may still have a rebellious nature that may cause you to do the opposite of what you are told to do, especially in your line of work.

You have a strong imagination, intuition and creativity which can be applied to any career of your choosing. Sudden changes in employment is probable and you may be better suited to being self-employed.

Routine work drives you to boredom. A career in electronics, computers, invention, metaphysics or mechanics is in harmony with your energy.

In the past you were a Seer, or healer, geomancer, priest or astronomer-astrologer priest. You have a great talent in metaphysics and in the distant past you once studied in the large libraries, for example, in Alexandria, and can tap into this knowledge by using mediation to gain a wealth of wisdom and deep understanding.

URANUS RETROGRADE MOTION

In a past life, you were forced to conform to working hard and long hours. You were probably bound to a location or may have been a slave. This memory has left you with the desire for total freedom, not to be bound by responsibility, or to work long and laborious hours. If you are forced to conform you will rebel. You need to find a way of expressing your creative and intuitive ideas and concepts in light of your karmic past.

SOUL GUIDANCE AND GUIDES

A soul lesson is to realise that your freedom is important to your Soul's evolution. You have an advanced and knowledgeable guide that will give you great advice and spiritual information. Your guide will also give you inspiration and deep insight which appears to come out of the blue or in unexpected ways. You resonate with the stars of Orion, Aquarius, and the beautifully bright star Vega.

NEPTUNE IN TENTH HOUSE
MALE OR FEMALE INCARNATION

Neptune at the time of your birth activated your spiritual body and throughout your many past lives you have been a powerful psychic or medium.

However, if you have Neptune in the tenth House, strange and confusing things happened to you in a past life with respect to your career and social standing. If you have experienced this in your current life, it is because your inner self is trying to steer you in a spiritual direction. Previously, in a life that you lived before this one, your public image may have had its ups and downs due to forces beyond your control.

In a past life you had strong idealism and you were artistic, inspirational, humanitarian and deeply psychic. Today, the theatre, chemistry, psychic activities, photography or dealings with health are possible career outlets.

Your karmic gift is your deep and far-reaching psychic ability. In a past life you were a Priest/ess.

There may be karmic residue influencing your life, due to a Soul Contract between you and your parents. This may manifest as a feeling of rejection by one or both parents. One of your parents may be unusual in some way, possibly psychic or working as an actor or singer. Forgiveness will dissipate the energy, loosen the bond, and free you and your parents of the karmic past.

NEPTUNE RETROGRADE MOTION

In a past life you were involved in a scandal or you were dishonest and this caused your downfall. In this life, it is really important for you to be open and honest. You need to express yourself in a creative manner and if you feel bound by too much responsibility, you may become unreliable.

You have inherited artistic and creative talent and if you fail to express it, you will feel frustrated and blocked. Your karmic gift is your deep and far-reaching psychic ability. In a past life you were a Seer or a Priest/ess.

SOUL GUIDANCE AND GUIDES

A soul lesson is to be open and honest. If you get confused, you need to ask for help to clarify your thoughts and ideas. You have a spiritual link to Neptune, the water spirits and to star systems such as Delphinus, Pisces and the Winged Horse, Pegasus, which is close to the celestial Fishes in the heavens. You have a psychic guide, possibly from Atlantis, Greece or Egypt that is always near you.

PLUTO IN TENTH HOUSE
MALE OR FEMALE INCARNATION

Pluto at the time of your birth activated your spiritual and psychic nature. You have the ability to see beyond the Third Dimension and into the ethers of time.

In a past life unforeseen activities affected your career or social standing in a dramatic way. The politics of an ancient society influenced your status and reputation in the world. That said, you were self-assertive and learnt to incorporate diplomacy and patience into your personality, especially when dealing with the world at large. You rose to a position of power and then felt a desire to retreat from society, or a desire to be of benefit and service to the community.

At one stage in this past life you used your power and force to get your way and it bought about your downfall. Thus, the karmic lesson is not to misuse your will and power. Your karmic gift is your ability to perceive the thoughts and feeling of others and sense deep and hidden undercurrents.

You have inherited the skills to uplift people and an instinct for knowing why people do the things they do.

PLUTO RETROGRADE MOTION

In a past life you felt alienated from others as you may have been imprisoned, or worked behind the scenes. A sense of desperation and aloneness was absorbed into the soul and into your DNA memory. If you have a sense that your life lacks something – the trace memory of alienation is resurfacing. As a result, you may feel that you have to stay in control or dictate to others what they should be doing.

Knowing that these inner traits are from a time that was, and letting go of them, will remove any blockage. You have incredible will and power as well as a sharp and perceptive mind.

SOUL GUIDANCE AND GUIDES

A soul lesson is to realise that you do not have to control other people or manipulate others. Learning to trust and communicate your feelings will allow age-old deep wounds to heal.

You have one of the most knowledgeable guides from a high realm that is close to you. You have a spiritual link to the Antares in Scorpio and deep space, such as other galaxies, and the Galactic Centre.

CHIRON IN THE TENTH HOUSE
MALE OR FEMALE INCARNATION

In a past life you were in a position of spiritual power, you may have been a leader, priest or healer of advanced knowledge and capability. You realised and understood your true purpose on the Earth plane. Deep within you there is immense wisdom and power.

Chiron in the tenth house activated your crown chakra at birth and gave you a sense of authority and power born of past experiences, though you may try to ignore that! Realise that you have great spiritual power, but if you fail to recognise this, the result may be conflicts in your inner most being. One healing solution is to accept the power inherent within you rather than to ignore it. You may experience health issues or conflicts around the time of the 'Saturn return', between the ages of 28 and 30.

In a past life, you were constantly pushed to achieve, which may have given you an aversion to success and power. The key to success is to tap into your spiritual power and the wealth of wisdom that you have within. The more you can identify with your spiritual power, the more satisfaction you will find.

CHIRON IN THE TENTH HOUSE
RETROGRADE MOTION. MALE INCARNATION

Chiron in the tenth house activated your crown chakra at birth giving you great spiritual power. You are a natural healer, writer and you are psychic, yet you tend to doubt your own gift and ability. This is because in a past life someone you healed lied and, for example, said you were useless and worthless. You believed his or her treacherous words and refused to heal anyone again. For some time you became a hermit.

In this life, you may doubt who you are and what you can do. There may have been someone in your past that put you down and made you feel that you could not achieve your goals.

Yet, you have immense will power to succeed and can dream your dreams awake. Trust your self, you come from a healing background with deep wisdom, and you are powerful.

SOUL GUIDANCE AND GUIDES

A soul lesson is to tap into your will and power. One of your spiritual guides is a healer. You have a special relationship to the stars of Sagittarius, Aquila the Eagle, Ursa Major and Arcturus.

Chapter Twelve
Druidic Soul Star Countries

*T*he association of the planets to particular countries was compiled by the astrologer, Claudius Ptolemy (cAD 100 - AD 170), who studied in Alexandria, Egypt. The ancient associations should be considered as a guideline only. A general and more broader planetary description is given which will allow the reader to determine the planetary attributes of any given village, town or city by association.

However, if a client feels a strong link to a particular country, or place, or you feel a genuine link to a particular place or country on behalf of your client, go with your feelings, as they are usually correct.

LOCATIONS ASSOCIATED WITH THE PLANETS

The Sun rules hot countries and deserts and all locations were kings have ruled or fought. For example, King Arthur's battlegrounds and feasting halls would come under the rulership of the Sun.

Cities: Rome, Prague, Philadelphia and modern day Los Angeles.

Countries: In the ancient world Chaldea, Phoenicia, Macedonia, Phrygia, Rome, France, Italy, Scilly, Romania, and the Bohemian Alps.

The Moon rules cold (or moist) countries, all lunar orientated temples and their cities, and the lost cities of Antarctica. The Moon resides over all locations where Queens have ruled, such as the legendary Queen Boudicca of the Iceni Celtic tribe, or the royal locations of Queen Cleopatra. Also, locations and places associated with the Mother Mary such as Lourdes in France.

Cities: Constantinople, Genoa, Algeria, Atlantis.

Countries: Scotland, Holland, some Native American locations in Canada, New Zealand, Northern Africa, and also Pacific Islands.

Mercury, generally speaking, rules temple spaces or libraries once used for the magical arts. The meeting places of two roads in towns and cities such as a crossroads, or places were trade and commerce occurred.

Cities: London, Melbourne, and modern day San Francisco.

Countries: Sardinia, North coast of Africa, Assyria, Aracdia, Babylonia, Mesopotamia, and some parts of Sumer. In the ancient world Lower Egypt, Flanders and Lombardy.

Venus generally speaking rules all feminine locations and temples dedicated to the goddess. Lands that have been associated with powerful women, or saints, such as the link to France through Joan of Arc and all locations associated with Mary Magdalene.

Cities: Manytua, Dublin, Lucerne, Leipsig, Lucerne.

Countries: Ireland, Russia, Crete, Persia, Egypt, Turkey – Ephesus. Switzerland. Ancient Peoples Egyptians, Druids in England, France, Ireland – the Celtic lands of old.

Mars generally speaking rules all masculine locations. For example, churches dedicated to a masculine saint, all war sites, battlegrounds and war locations, from Native American battles to WWII sites.

Cities: Naples, ancient Athens, and Sparta, Washington DC, Florence.

Countries: England, Germany, Palestine, Catalonia, Morocco, Algeria, Syria, and Libya. Ancient people ruled by Mars, Jews and Moslems.

Jupiter rules religious organisations and educational places, such as the Vatican. Also, locations that were associated with higher education such as the long lost Druidic Cors (Colleges) or the temple colleges of Egypt or Sumer.

Cites: Cologne, Toledo, Budapest, York, Avalon, Avignon, Stuttgart and Nottingham.

Countries: Spain, Hungary, West Indies, Easter Island, parts of Egypt, Dalmatia, Moravia and Provence. Manilius states that countries associated with Jupiter's ruler, Sagittarius, are Crete and Latium.

Saturn rules all long lost ancient civilisations that time has forgot which are associated with disciplined rulers or large organisations.

Cities: Oxford, Brussels, Delhi, Port Said, and administration centres of most cities come under this influence.

Countries: Modern parts of Greece, Ethiopia, Albania, Lithuania, Bulgaria, Afghanistan, Mexico and India. In the ancient world Macedonia, Illyria, Thrace, Greece, Afghanistan, Mexico, and Stonehenge.

Uranus rules locations that are bohemian, radical and different. Uranus was not discovered until 1718. Therefore, any locations associated with Uranus are not derived from traditional sources and relate to Aquarius, the constellation that Uranus rules.

Cities: Hamburg, Leningrad, Peking, Bremen, Salzburg, Trent and Stockholm.

Countries: Ethiopia, Russia, parts of South America, parts of Australia, Bohemia (Czech Republic), Prussia , Lithuania, Sweden, Canada, and parts of Arabia and Poland.

Neptune rules all long lost cities and temples that have been reclaimed by the sea such as Atlantis and Doggerland. Neptune also rules coastal ports, fishing villages and towns. Neptune was not discovered until September 23rd 1846 and so the listed locations are not derived from traditional sources but relate to Pisces, the constellation that Neptune rules.

Cities: Alexandria, Seville, Compostela, Worm, Lancaster.

Countries: Portugal, Normandy, Atlantis, Upper Egypt (Nubia), Galicia (in Northern Spain) and Calabria. Neptune rules Atlantis. In the city centre there was once a shrine dedicated to Neptune and two springs, one hot and one cold.

Pluto rules all locations that are underground such as mines, or temple spaces that are deep below ground, for example, like Malta's hypogeum, tunnels beneath pyramid structures, Neolithic long barrows, such as West Kennet long barrow near Avebury, or darkened enclosed spaces. Pluto was not discovered until 1930 and so the listed locations are not derived from traditional sources but relate to Scorpio, the constellation that Pluto rules.

Cities: Valencia, Fez, Messina, parts of London, Dover, Liverpool, New Orleans, Baltimore, Cincinnati, Milwaukee, Halifax and parts of Washington DC.

Countries: Norway, Catalonia, parts of Germany, and Northern Europe, Lemuria, Old China, Mauritania, Northern Sardinia.

Chiron rules all healing temples especially those in the Mediterranean.

Greece, Athens, India, China. All lost cities and ancient civilisations connected to healing.

Chapter Thirteen
Exploring Past Lives Through Meditation And Healing Techniques

Past life memories can also be accessed using meditation and visualization techniques. After a Druidic Soul Star reading it may benefit the client to try the following techniques. Try them yourself and explore the various techniques with an open-heart mind.

MEDITATION

Past life regression therapists often use mediation in their professional practices. A guided meditation encourages the client to explore their past lives and to access Soul memories in a relaxed and calm manner.

USING MEDITATION AND CREATIVE VISUALISATION

This simple exercise guides your unconscious mind, the Higher Self, which contains all the memories of your childhood, and past lives, to access information that is stored deep within the Soul.

Meditation is an easy way to enhance your awareness of past life memories, as it clears the mind of daily events, and mundane matters, allowing deep Soul memories to rise to consciousness.

Meditation also brings contentment, peace and harmony, which can help maintain physical, emotional and mental health. Meditation brings clarity and focus and you can tap into the 'true present' rather than contemplating the future. Meditation teaches you to control the mind and the emotions.

There is no right or wrong way to meditate. Whenever you are relaxed and your mind is 'still' you are in a meditative state. To meditate you can lie down or sit on a chair, or the floor, whatever makes you feel comfortable. It is easy to meditate. During meditation you will be receptive and experience inner awareness. You can talk your client through the process which is described below.

A PAST LIFE MEDITATION TECHNIQUE

Find a quiet place where you feel secure and safe.

Simply close you eyes and begin to focus on your breathing.

Breathe slowly and deeply until your breathing settles down into a calm and peaceful fashion.

Imagine, visualize or simply sense that you are surrounded by a beautiful blue, pink or white light. See this light all around you, like being in a bubble. This loving and all-healing light protects you.

Pay attention once more to your breathing. Breathe slowly and deeply. Become aware of your thoughts and gently let them go...

Do not get impatient or frustrated. Simply observe your thoughts a bit like watching the TV.

- In your mind go back in time to a happy adult memory and relive the memory. See the people, or event, clearly and with as much detail as you can. Remember what you were wearing, whom you were with, where you were and how you felt. Use your senses to hear, see, and recall smells to fully immerse yourself into the memory. *If you are guiding a person, take a long pause so the memories can be fully experienced.*
- Just let that memory fade now and take a nice deep breath.
- Now recall a childhood memory and relive that memory as clearly as you can... Remember where you were, what you were doing, what you were wearing, whom you were with and use your sense to hear, see and recall smells to fully immerse yourself into the memory. *If you are guiding a person, take a long pause so the memories can be fully experienced.*
- Let that memory fade and gently ask your Higher Self to show you a life that you lived before this one. Let thoughts naturally come and go... *Take a long pause.*
- Discuss the experience.
- Alternatively, visualise yourself in a different time. Let images

naturally flow into your conscious mind. If the material feels right and natural, it is coming from your unconscious mind. Do not analyse the images. Just observe them. How do they feel?

• Record all of the images, thoughts and feelings.

ALPHA BRAIN WAVES

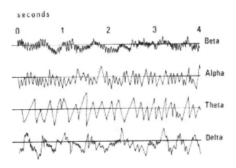

As your mind and body relaxes, the brain's electrical activity slows down and you will enter an alpha state, or even a theta state. Here, the 'electric wave activity' of the brain decreases to a much slower pace. Beta is the normal waking state.

USING DREAMS FOR PAST LIFE RECALL

Dreams can often contain clues about past lives. Upon waking, lie quietly and try not to move, be still. Gently recall your dream. Go over it in your mind. Then go over it again recalling more detail. Give your dream a title, as this helps to identify the theme.

KEEP A DREAM DIARY

Writing the details of your dream will stimulate your memory. Record all of your dreams in a 'dream diary'. Also, dream recall will improve in the future by following these simple, yet highly effective steps.

IN YOUR DREAM

Are you wearing different clothes? Are you in a different time? Ask yourself, do the details of your dreams interrelate or are they random?

Meditate upon certain aspects or details of your dreams. Focus your mind on the dream images. Visualise the image/content. Expand on the detail. Try not to inhibit your impressions mentally. Do not censor them.

It is common to receive a collection of past life fragments from different dreams which do not seem to make sense. Be patient and explore them all, especially the ones you are strongly drawn to. Use your intuition and feelings to guide you.

SELF OBSERVATION AND THE HOME

Look around your home, are you attracted to a particular era? Some people are attracted to the art or furniture of a particular period which may hint at Soul memories of lives that have been lived before this one.

Ask your client about their home. Are they drawn to a particular era reflected in their furniture, paintings, etc...?

BIRTHMARKS

Birthmarks often indicate past life trauma, so ask your client if they have any birthmarks or red patches. This may indicate past life residue which is stored psychic energy that identifies a particular area on the physical body, which has experienced trauma.

HEALING AND RELEASING

If during the Druidic Soul Star reading your client has experienced an emotional past life, you can employ a healing technique to determine if the emotion or trauma is still influencing the aura or physical body. You can do this by using a psychic 'scanning' method that scans the body to see *where* the trauma or psychic energy may be residing. Quite often past life psychic residue will stay in the auric field or physical body for centuries. Psychic scanning can find the location so that the energy can be released.

SCANNING AND HEALING

Ask the client to choose his or her own personal healing colour. Encourage the chose of a positive colour and never black, brown, grey or red. Vibrant and beautiful colours make great energetic healing tools. Make a note of the chosen colour.

A great way of scanning the body is to use a psychic 'hoop' to scan the body and auric field and it is an easy technique to employ. Most people can imagine or visualize a 'hula-hoop' which they may have seen, or used, during their childhood. Alternatively, encourage the client to imagine, visualize or sense a large circle of light above their head. Draw an example for the client if they are unsure of what they should be visualizing.

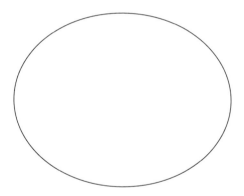

- Ask the client to close their eyes and imagine, visualize or simply sense a spiritual light hoop, a circle of light, in the colour they have chosen. The hoop is above their head and encourage the client to make the hoop large enough so that it is about 10 inches either side of their physical body.
- Ask the client to imagine, visualize, or sense, the hoop slowly descending from just above the top of the head to their feet. Repeat the process a few times so that the client becomes familiar with how easy the process is.
- Explain to the client that this is a psychic scanning process. When the hoop is used for clearing, it will naturally stop at an area which requires healing. If the hoop stops, you should verbally encourage the client to imagine, visualize or sense

radiant coloured light being released by the coloured light hoop. The light will be magnetically absorbed into the aura and into the body – right down to the cellular level. You need to encourage the client to sense the coloured light being drawn into their body, naturally and easily. If necessary, repeat this process several times. Alchemically, releasing and transmuting any psychic residue or trauma, this form of colour healing fills the body with all-healing love and light. It is a rewarding and relaxing experience.

KARMA CLEANSING RITUAL
PART 1

1. Look at your life is there something that is causing you concern?

Write down your true feelings about the situation. What physically upsets you? What emotionally upsets you? What mentally upsets you? What gives you the darkest or saddest feelings around this situation? Find the 'pain points' and really explore them, so you can fully understand them and why they need to be released.

2. Look into your past and see where you find similar situations or feelings. Look for patterns.

If you find patterns of problem behavior, or repetitive situations in this life, you have probably carried them over from a past life; and will carry them into the next one. This is the karma that needs to be released.

3. Meditate upon the pattern, with the intention of unlocking the details of how this concerns your current life.

4. Once you have looked into the issue, learned all you can about it, accepted and taken responsibility for your role, feel that you understand the lessons and you know what needs to be released, you can heal the issue by simply acknowledge the prevailing pattern or energy (for example, inferiority, lack of esteem, poverty issues etc)…

Ask the Universe, Father Mother God, or how you see the God Source, to have the issues from both the past and present lives released.

THE FIRST AND MOST
IMPORTANT ACTION IS FORGIVENESS

Asking for forgiveness from the higher self of those you've wronged, forgiving those that have wronged you, and also forgiving yourself, is the first step towards healing the past.

Other actions might involve anything from changing jobs, addressing relationship issues, or making lifestyle changes. It's all about creating change and taking action; action is what matters the most.

Make sure that, whatever you decide to do, you are doing it with the best, highest and purest intention. Know that these intentions and their actions are changing the course of your karma, your life.

The second thing you can do is a releasing ritual to make the release more real for you.

KARMA CLEANSING RITUAL
PART 2

On a piece of paper write what needs to be released. If you have more than one issue, it's a good idea to use a small slip of paper for each issue. Find somewhere safe which is outdoors, where you can go and bring your slips of paper, a fireproof container, a smudge stick, (or loose sage), a lighter or matches and a small container of water.

Light each slip of paper on fire, one at a time and say:

*"I release (what you have written down) **this karma and open new paths to living my life."***

Let the paper burn, doing this for each slip of paper you have. When you have burned them all, make sure the ashes are cooled and bury them. *Really feel the energy leaving you.*

Then break off a little of the sage from the stick and sprinkle it on the earth as a thank you, light the bundle and smudge yourself. As you do this say, *"I am free from the past and I face my future anew."*

Now dip your finger into the container of water so that it is damp and gently press the dap water against your heart chakra. And say: *'I am fully cleansed by the four sacred elements of Fire, Earth, Air and Water. I welcome new opportunities into my life so that I may live a rewarding, giving and loving life'.*

The Four Elements were used in this sacred rite. Fire – burning the paper, Earth – burying the ashes, Air – smudging with smoke and Water – pressed against the heart chakra.

CONCLUDING COMMENTS

You now have all the key skills to become a Druidic Soul Star past life reader. You can cast a chart, interpret the karmic houses and recognise that each planet represents a past life. The Soul Star chart is a spiritual tool which encourages your own Sixth Sense to develop and assist in interpreting the various past lives.

The chart shows you the most important past lives and describes in detail the individual's spiritual heritage. You may recognise a 'theme' that flows through the chart identifying particular karmic traits or behavioural issues which can be seen and understood. Also, you can offer some healing techniques that can help release karmic energy or stored trauma.

I suggest that you begin to practice this ancient art on friends and family. Your confidence will soon grow and you will be able to advertise your services as a past life reader and interpreter.

If you are interested in becoming a fully qualified Druidic Soul Star past life reader, you can take a professional Druidic Soul Star course with www.EsotericCollege.com.

EsotericCollege.com was founded by Maria Wheatley who teaches on line courses combined with personal Skype lessons. The Druidic Soul Star Astrology course is closely based on this book. Contact mariawheatley@aol.com for details. All of our courses are fully affiliated with ABCC The Association of British Correspondence Colleges. Maria offers personal Druidic Soul Star readings - email mariawheatley@aol.com for details.

ESOTERIC COLLEGE

ONLINE RESOURCES

www.horoscopeswithin.com

www.alabe.com

www.theaveburyexperience.co.uk

www.EsotericCollege.com for on line and Skype courses on Dowsing, Tarot, Past Life Regression, Druidic Soul Star Astrology, Working with Gaia's Inner Waters to heal and Pendulum Dowsing for Health and Well-being.

RECOMMENDED AUTHORS

Transcendental Astrology
by A.G.S. Norris

Alan Oken Completer Astrology

Robert Hand Planets in Transit

BLANK DRUIDIC SOUL STAR CHART

About the Author

*A*uthor and professional dowser Maria Wheatley has been studying dowsing, astrology and past lives for over 20 years. Maria is considered a leading authority on earth energies and has spent the past ten years researching how ley lines and earth energies were integrated into ancient sites, and more importantly, how they were harnessed by our ancient ancestor to raise consciousness.

Maria Wheatley has been teaching subjects such as Earth Divination, the symbolic language of Mother Earth, and dowsing since 1992 and is the founder of EsotericCollege.com. Maria has been raising awareness of how the Earth's energetic eco-system can enhance or hinder our lives. She teaches corporate companies in the UK and a US nursing college how to identify the Earth's healing lines and geodetic patterns and to negate inharmonious energies.

Maria's late father, Dennis Wheatley, was considered one of Britain's most advanced dowsers who taught several well-known authors, such as Geoff Stray, to dowse the hidden energies that flow silently through the Earth. The way forward is to work with the Earth not against her. Maria has studied Bardic Druidry with the BDO and is a practising Druid bringing back the Old Wise Ways to heal the Earth and one another.

If you liked this book, you might also like:

Dancing Forever with Spirit
by Garnet Schulhauser
The Three Waves of Volunteers and the New Earth
by Dolores Cannon
Raising Our Vibrations
by Sherri Cortland
Feng Shui From the Inside, Out
by Victoria Pendragon
The Convoluted Universe, Book 1-4
by Dolores Cannon
Let's Get Natural with Herbs
by Debra Rayburn
Out of the Archives – Earth Changes
by Aron Abrahamsen

For more information about any of the above titles, soon to be released titles,
or other items in our catalog, write, phone or visit our website:
Ozark Mountain Publishing, LLC
PO Box 754, Huntsville, AR 72740
479-738-2348
www.ozarkmt.com

For more information about any of the titles published by Ozark Mountain Publishing, Inc., soon to be released titles, or other items in our catalog, write, phone or visit our website:

Ozark Mountain Publishing, Inc.

PO Box 754

Huntsville, AR 72740

479-738-2348/800-935-0045

www.ozarkmt.com

Dolores Cannon
A Soul Remembers Hiroshima
Between Death and Life
Conversations with Nostradamus,
    Volume I, II, III
The Convoluted Universe -Book One,
    Two, Three, Four, Five
The Custodians
Five Lives Remembered
Jesus and the Essenes
Keepers of the Garden
Legacy from the Stars
The Legend of Starcrash
The Search for Hidden Sacred Knowledge
They Walked with Jesus
The Three Waves of Volunteers and the
    New Earth
Aron Abrahamsen
Holiday in Heaven
Out of the Archives – Earth Changes
Justine Alessi & M. E. McMillan
Rebirth of the Oracle
Kathryn/Patrick Andries
Naked in Public
Kathryn Andries
The Big Desire
Dream Doctor
Soul Choices: Six Paths to Find Your Life
    Purpose
Soul Choices: Six Paths to Fulfilling
    Relationships
Patrick Andries
Owners Manual for the Mind
Tom Arbino
You Were Destined to be Together
Rev. Keith Bender
The Despiritualized Church
Dan Bird
Waking Up in the Spiritual Age
O.T. Bonnett, M.D./Greg Satre
Reincarnation: The View from Eternity
What I Learned After Medical School
Why Healing Happens
Julia Cannon
Soul Speak – The Language of Your Body
Ronald Chapman
Seeing True
Albert Cheung
The Emperor's Stargate
Jack Churchward
Lifting the Veil on the Lost Continent of
    Mu
The Stone Tablets of Mu
Sherri Cortland
Guide Group Fridays
Raising Our Vibrations for the New Age

Spiritual Tool Box
Windows of Opportunity
Cinnamon Crow
Chakra Zodiac Healing Oracle
Teen Oracle
Michael Dennis
Morning Coffee with God
God's Many Mansions
Claire Doyle Beland
Luck Doesn't Happen by Chance
Jodi Felice
The Enchanted Garden
Max Flindt/Otto Binder
Mankind: Children of the Stars
Arun & Sunanda Gandhi
The Forgotten Woman
Maiya & Geoff Gray-Cobb
Angels -The Guardians of Your Destiny
Seeds of the Soul
Carolyn Greer Daly
Opening to Fullness of Spirit
Julia Hanson
Awakening to Your Creation
Donald L. Hicks
The Divinity Factor
Anita Holmes
Twidders
Antoinette Lee Howard
Journey Through Fear
Vara Humphreys
The Science of Knowledge
Victoria Hunt
Kiss the Wind
James H. Kent
Past Life Memories as A Confederate
    Soldier
Mandeep Khera
Why?
Dorothy Leon
Is Jehovah an E.T
Mary Letorney
Discover the Universe Within You
Diane Lewis
From Psychic to Soul
Sture Lönnerstrand
I Have Lived Before
Donna Lynn
From Fear to Love
Irene Lucas
Thirty Miracles in Thirty Days
Susan Mack & Natalia Krawetz
My Teachers Wear Fur Coats
Patrick McNamara
Beauty and the Priest
Maureen McGill
Baby It's You

Other Books by Ozark Mountain Publishing, Inc.

Maureen McGill & Nola Davis
Live from the Other Side
Henry Michaelson
And Jesus Said – A Conversation
Dennis Milner
Kosmos
Andy Myers
Not Your Average Angel Book
Guy Needler
Avoiding Karma
Beyond the Source – Book 1, Book 2
The Anne Dialogues
The History of God
The Origin Speaks
James Nussbaumer
The Master of Everything
Mastering Your Own Spiritual Freedom
Sherry O'Brian
Peaks and Valleys
Riet Okken
The Liberating Power of Emotions
John Panella
The Gnostic Papers
Victor Parachin
Sit a Bit
Nikki Pattillo
A Spiritual Evolution
Children of the Stars
Rev. Grant H. Pealer
A Funny Thing Happened on the
    Way to Heaven
Worlds Beyond Death
Karen Peebles
The Other Side of Suicide
Victoria Pendragon
Born Healers
Feng Shui from the Inside, Out
Sleep Magic
Michael Perlin
Fantastic Adventures in Metaphysics
Walter Pullen
Evolution of the Spirit
Christine Ramos, RN
A Journey into Being
Debra Rayburn
Let's Get Natural with Herbs
Charmian Redwood
A New Earth Rising
Coming Home to Lemuria
David Rivinus
Always Dreaming

Briceida Ryan
The Ultimate Dictionary of Dream
    Language
M. Don Schorn
Elder Gods of Antiquity
Legacy of the Elder Gods
Gardens of the Elder Gods
Reincarnation...Stepping Stones of Life
Garnet Schulhauser
Dance of Eternal Rapture
Dance of Heavenly Bliss
Dancing Forever with Spirit
Dancing on a Stamp
Annie Stillwater Gray
Education of a Guardian Angel
The Dawn Book
Work of a Guardian Angel
Blair Styra
Don't Change the Channel
Natalie Sudman
Application of Impossible Things
L.R. Sumpter
We Are the Creators
Dee Wallace/Jarrad Hewett
The Big E
Dee Wallace
Conscious Creation
James Wawro
Ask Your Inner Voice
Janie Wells
Embracing the Human Journey
Payment for Passage
Dennis Wheatley/ Maria Wheatley
The Essential Dowsing Guide
Maria Wheatley
Druidic Soul Star Astrology
Jacquelyn Wiersma
The Zodiac Recipe
Sherry Wilde
The Forgotten Promise
Lyn Willmoth
A Small Book of Comfort
Stuart Wilson & Joanna Prentis
Atlantis and the New Consciousness
Beyond Limitations
The Essenes -Children of the Light
The Magdalene Version
Power of the Magdalene
Robert Winterhalter
The Healing Christ

For more information about any of the above titles, soon to be released titles,
or other items in our catalog, write, phone or visit our website:
PO Box 754, Huntsville, AR 72740
479-738-2348/800-935-0045
www.ozarkmt.com